ELEMENTS OF
BASE PAY
ADMINISTRATION

Jason C. Kovac, CCP, CBP
L. Kate Beatty, CCP
Executive Editors

About WorldatWork®

WorldatWork (www.worldatwork.org) is the association for human resources professionals focused on attracting, motivating and retaining employees. Founded in 1955, WorldatWork provides practitioners with knowledge leadership to effectively implement total rewards — compensation, benefits, work-life, performance and recognition, development and career opportunities — by connecting employee engagement to business performance. WorldatWork supports its 30,000 members and customers in 30 countries with thought leadership, education, publications, research and certification.

The WorldatWork group of registered marks includes: WorldatWork®, workspan®, Certified Compensation Professional or CCP®, Certified Benefits Professional® or CBP, Global Remuneration Professional or GRP®, Work-Life Certified Professional or WLCP™, WorldatWork Society of Certified Professionals®, and Alliance for Work-Life Progress® or AWLP®.

Any laws, regulations or other legal requirements noted in this publication are, to the best of the publisher's knowledge, accurate and current as of this book's publishing date. WorldatWork is providing this information with the understanding that WorldatWork is not engaged, directly or by implication, in rendering legal, accounting or other related professional services. You are urged to consult with an attorney, accountant or other qualified professional concerning your own specific situation and any questions that you may have related to that.

This book is published by WorldatWork. The interpretations, conclusions and recommendations in this book are those of the author and do not necessarily represent those of WorldatWork.

© 2006 WorldatWork
ISBN 1-57963-1568 (Paperback/softback)
 978-157963-271-7 (E-book)

No portion of this publication may be reproduced in any form without express written permission from WorldatWork.

The Total Rewards Association
WorldatWork Press
www.worldatwork.org

Acknowledgments

WorldatWork Press would like to thank the following technical reviewers for helping to shape and strengthen the content of this book:

Jennifer C. Loftus, CCP, CBP, GRP, SPHR, National Director, *Astron Solutions*

Charles Pascual, CCP, Executive Director, Compensation and Benefits, *Catalina Marketing Corporation*

Patricia Zingheim, Ph.D., Partner, *Schuster-Zingheim & Associates Inc.*

Article Reviewers

Michael Batt, President, *USAlliance Consulting*

Tom Farmer, Senior Consultant, *Hewitt Associates*

Nancy S. Fraser, CCP, Director, Global Compensation, Benefits & HRIS, *Sykes Enterprises Inc.*

Doug A. Grieser, CCP, Senior Manager, Compensation and Benefits, *Insight Distribution Network Inc.*

Matthew Harper, CCP, Executive Compensation Manager, *MeadWestvaco*

Linda K. Ison, CCP, Managing Director, *Mercer Human Resource Consulting*

Richard D. Landsberg, *Nationwide Financial Services*

Bruce G. Lawson, CCP, President, *Fox Lawson & Associates LLC*

Jim McKay, FFA, ASA, M&A Engagement Leader, *Watson Wyatt Worldwide*

Howard Pardue, SPHR, Vice President, Human Resources, *Western University of Health Sciences*

Mark E. Pittel, CCP, Managing Director, *Sullivan Cotter & Associates Inc.*

James P. Saik, CCP, CHRP, Manager, Total Compensation, *UFA Co-Operative Limited*

Michael Schelstrate, CCP, SPHR, Human Resources Director, *Triumph Composite Systems Inc.*

Bruce Schlegel, Director, Compensation, Benefits & HRIS, *Xilinx Inc.*

Jeremy B. Sochol, CCP, Vice President, HR Shared Services, *Standard Register Co.*

Bruce I. Spiegel, Vice President, Global Compensation Services, *ACS Inc.*

Gary E. Starzmann, CCP, CBP, GRP, SPHR, Global Compensation Solutions Architect, *ACS Inc.*

Mark Szypko, CCP, Director, Compensation, Benefits & HRIS, *Comcast Corp.*

WorldatWork Staff Contributors

Dan Cafaro

Rebecca Williams

Alan Luu

Wendy McMorine

Kris Sotelo

Table of Contents

Chapter 1 – Compensation Program Objectives 1
Figure 1-1: Total Rewards Model 6
Figure 1-2: Seven Categories of Work-Life Effectiveness 7

Chapter 2 – Legal and Regulatory Environments 11
Sherman Anti-Trust Act 13
Davis-Bacon Act 14
National Labor Relations Act 14
Walsh-Healey Act 14
Fair Labor Standards Act 14
- Minimum Wage 15
- Overtime Pay 15
Exemption 19
Salary Basis 20
Salary Limit 20
Duties Tests 20
Child Labor Provisions 22
Recordkeeping 22
FLSA Enforcement 23
Service Contract Act 23
Anti-Discrimination Laws 23
- Equal Pay Act 24
- Title VII of the Civil Rights Act 25
- Age Discrimination in Employment Act 25
- Executive Order 11246 26
- Vocation Rehabilitation Act of 1973 27
- Vietnam Era Veterans Readjustment Act of 1974 27
- Americans with Disabilities Act 27

Chapter 3 – The Job Process 29

Job Analysis 31
Figure 3-1: Building a Base Pay Structure 32
Job Documentation 34
Job Documentation Components 35
Other Job Description Considerations 36
Developing the Job Worth Hierarchy 36
Market Pricing 37
Job Content Evaluation Methods 38
Nonquantitative – "Whole Job" Evaluation 38
Quantitative – "Factor" Evaluation 39
Factor Selection and Weighting 39
Who Should Perform the Evaluation 40
Other Considerations 40
Pay-Data Collection and Analysis 41
- Pay-Data Collection 41
- Figure 3-2: Sample Labor Market – Large Retail Firm 42
- Analysis of the Collected Market Data 43

Chapter 4 – Base Pay Structure 45

Setting Rates and/or Ranges for Jobs 47
Figure 4-1: Market Position – Lead 47
Figure 4-2: Market Position – Lag 48
Figure 4-3: Market Position – Lead/Lag 48
Pay Structure 49
Figure 4-4: Pay Range 50
Figure 4-5: Red and Green Circle Rates 51
Broadbanding 52
Sidebar: Broadbanding is not for Everyone 53
Starting Rates of Pay 54
Increases to Base Rates of Pay 54
Merit Pay Considerations 56
Performance Appraisal Considerations 57

Chapter 5 – Communication of the Pay Program 59

Staying on Top of Program Administration 62
Checklist: Subjects Frequently Included 63

Chapter 6 – Maintaining and Auditing the Pay Program 65

Keys to Successful Pay-Program Maintenance 67
Ongoing Administrative Activities 67
Pay-Program Audits 68

Chapter 7 – Current Trends 73
Hot Skills 75
Target Market Position 76
Access to Salary Data 76
Sidebar: Reliability of Today's Sources 76
Performance Differentiation 77

Articles & Perspectives 79
Compensation Philosophy: The Starting Point 81
    Christopher Kelley and David Gustat
What Is Base Salary? 86
    Michael O'Malley, Ph.D.
Market Pricing 101: The Science and the Art 94
    Deb Grigson, John Delaney and Robert Jones, JD, CPA, CEBS
Linking Compensation Policies and Programs to Organizational Effectiveness ... 102
    Dow Scott, Ph.D., Richard S. Sperling, CCP, Thomas D. McMullen
    and Marc Wallace
New Ways to Manage Pay: Upgrading Base Pay, Pay Progression
    and Variable Pay Plans to Attract and Retain Talent 114
    N. Frederic Crandall, Ph.D.
Compensation in the Hot Seat 121
    John M. Bremen
The Future of Compensation Professionals, According to Your Colleagues 128
    Barbara Manny, Thomas D. McMullen, Richard S. Sperling, CCP,
    and Dow Scott, Ph.D.

Glossary 135

Selected References 151

Compensation Program Objectives 1

Throughout history, employers have struggled with how to attract, motivate and retain their workforce. What if I give them more base pay? More pay-at-risk or incentive pay? Better health insurance? Pension? 401(k)? Flexible work schedules? How can I provide something of value to the employees, so that they will stay with the organization and increase productivity? This value comes in the form of total rewards.

One of the main components of the total rewards model is compensation. Compensation can be defined as the cash provided by an employer to an employee for services rendered. Compensation comprises the elements of pay (for example, base pay, variable pay, stock, etc.) that an employer offers an employee in return for his or her services. Compensation is just one of the many means an employer has to attract, retain and motivate employees.

Organizations need to determine where base pay fits within the business strategy. The first step in determining this is to understand the organizational compensation philosophy and strategy. Not all organizations have a written philosophy or strategy but those that do can ensure their compensation programs closely align to the business strategy. When creating a compensation philosophy/strategy, the main goal of the statements should be to ensure the compensation programs will support the business goals. For example, if the business goals are to increase sales by 15 percent, but the compensation programs do not motivate employees to achieve those goals, the compensation plan is broken.

A major component to compensation philosophy/strategy development is to create compensation program objectives. The following list contains some of the most common compensation program objectives:

- Internally equitable
- Externally competitive
- Affordable
- Fiscally responsible
- Understandable
- Legal/defensible
- Efficient to administer

- Flexible
- Culturally appropriate
- Aligned with business objectives.

The most common objectives of a compensation program are to be internally equitable and externally competitive. Each organization needs to determine which objectives are most important and prioritize them. It is vital to select objectives that support the compensation philosophy/strategy and that link to the business strategy. If the objectives are not aligned, the compensation program will not help the organization achieve its business objectives.

These compensation objectives may be altered based on changes in the business strategy. A key component in determining the appropriate objectives is to recognize where the organization is in the business life cycle. For organizations in the startup phase, affordability is typically a key objective, with greater emphasis on incentives than base salary. As the organization moves into the growth stage, external equity might take a more prominent role in addition to being more flexible to attract, retain and motivate employees. When the organization moves into the maturity phase, base pay might move more to an internal equity-driven approach for some key positions and an externally competitive approach for others. At this stage organizations are looking to have the plan more efficient to administer and are creating incentive programs to achieve business objectives. As the organization moves into the decline stage, base pay has the potential to be frozen, with incentives being used to motivate employees. At this stage, organizations might be more concerned with being legal/defensible and affordable. These are just some examples of how the business life cycle could influence the compensation objectives. Organizations move in and out of phases in the continuum, and it is important to recognize what stage the organization is in and utilize the appropriate tools for that life cycle.

When developing a compensation philosophy/strategy, organizations need to also review their total rewards strategy and determine how compensation fits within the organization's total rewards package. As stated previously, total rewards are a way to look at the entire employee value proposition for an organization. Total rewards encompass compensation, benefits, work-life initiatives, performance and recognition, as well as development and career opportunities. By looking at all of the aspects as one, and recognizing that each component feeds into attracting, retaining and motivating employees, organizations will better understand the employee value proposition. Determining where and how compensation fits into this model is key to any successful compensation program.

Compensation and benefits professionals have come a long way since serving as a hybrid job between human resources and finance. Salary structures then were very rigid and highly controlled, and benefits programs were designed as a one-size-fits-all answer to a homogenous workforce. Today compensation and benefits are considered a recognized profession. Since the 1970s, organizations have put a greater emphasis on strategically designed direct compensation and benefits programs. These programs have become more flexible and adaptable to the ever-changing work environment and reflect the following:

- Emergence of greater international/multinational organizational presence
- Influx of new generations of employees (generation X, Y, etc.) with different values
- Increased business competition
- Workforce diversification, addition of two-income households and the decline of the sole breadwinner model
- Stricter government regulations and mandates for compensation and benefits (e.g., Fair Labor Standards Act of 1938, Employee Retirement Income Security Act of 1974, Sarbanes-Oxley Act of 2002)
- Health-care cost increases and the desire to contain those increases while still providing health-care benefits to the workforce
- Health-care programs designed to cater to the changing demographics and needs of the workforce
- Perception of HR as more of a strategic partner
- Addition of work-life effectiveness programs in recognition of the changing needs of the workforce demographics.

Throughout the past decade, the professions of compensation and benefits have continued to advance and mature. As more strategic plans and designs are required for the changing workforce, additional stress and pressure have been placed on the compensation and benefits practitioners to find innovative ways to attract, retain and motivate employees. Based upon these needs, a new model has been introduced in these fields — a model of total rewards. Organizations that understand the concept as it affects their industry, competitive environment and employees, as well as know the proper way to deploy critical factors to their strategic advantage, will be the clear winners in the battle to attract, retain and motivate top performers.

Total rewards has five main components: (See Figure 1-1 on page 6.)

- Compensation
- Benefits
- Work-Life
- Performance and Recognition
- Development and Career Opportunities.

Compensation and benefits are the two core components of total rewards that address employee financial needs. In every organization there is some overlap of these components; the degree of overlap depends on the organizational culture and specific strategic program design. Each area has a distinct and unique body of

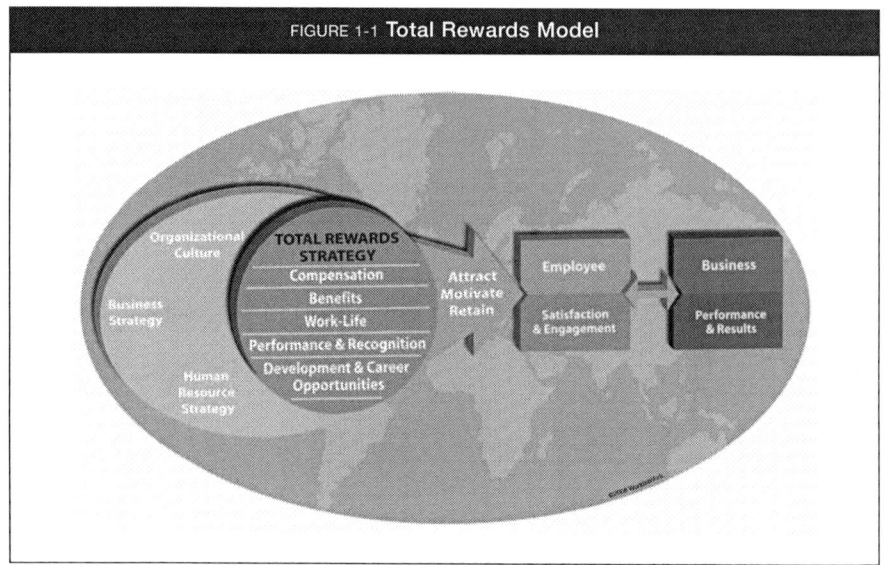

FIGURE 1-1 **Total Rewards Model**

knowledge. Individually and collectively, these components can assist the practitioner in addressing the needs of attraction, retention and motivation.

A third overlapping component is work-life. Unlike compensation and benefits, work-life is just beginning to move from a "field" to developing into a profession. Work-life addresses the nature of work and the many elements of rewards that are important to employees and employers, but are often less tangible than compensation and benefits. It is important to note that work-life overlaps and typically integrates with compensation and benefits.

While work-life elements have always existed in organizations, these elements have not always received much attention in the quest to attract, motivate and retain employees. However, research has consistently shown that employees place an extremely high value on matters that relate specifically to the total experience of working. (See Figure 1-2 on page 7.)

Each of these elements must be taken into consideration as part of the reasons why employees would want to work for an organization, why they would want to stay and what would energize them to perform at their best (attraction, motivation and retention). It's a matter of moving from employment to engagement.

The other two components of the total rewards model are performance and recognition and development and career opportunities. Performance can be used in many ways within an organization and is defined as follows:

- The alignment and assessment of organizational, team and individual efforts in the achievement of business goals.

FIGURE 1-2 Seven Categories of Work-Life Effectiveness

- **Dependent care**
  Caring for dependents can be defined as programs created that allow an employee to care for a person who relies on another for support. In most cases dependent refer to the following:
  - Child/children
  - Child/children of domestic partners
  - Elder
  - Adult with disabilities
  - Pets
- **Health and wellness support**
  Supporting health and wellness is defined as programs that provide for or maintain freedom from disease and provide for an optimal state of soundness of body and mind.
- **Workplace flexibility**
  Workplace flexibility was initiated on an ad-hoc basis to meet the needs of individual employees in particular situations. Eventually, when the value became evident, companies began more structured flexibility initiatives as a means to meet workforce business objectives. But flexibility is more than programs; it often requires a significant cultural shift for an organization.
- **Financial support programs**
  In the area of financial support, work-life is primarily concerned with gaining approval for — and helping implement — voluntary financial benefits and resources and referrals that assist employees with managing their financial responsibilities.
- **Creative use of paid and unpaid time off**
  This is defined as personal time away from work for family, relaxation, education, volunteerism, emergencies or military service. Some of the newer policies in this category include paid family leave for new fathers as well as mothers, and paid or release time for community service.
- **Community involvement programs**
  These programs involve not only external community outreach, such as company giving (foundations or direct), but also a renewed focus on building a strong internal sense of community. Formal ethics programs and shared (or catastrophic) programs, such as leave banks and disaster relief funds, are some of the creative new ways of taking care of each other.
- **Culture-change initiatives**
  Building such an effective, rewarding work environment always requires the buy-in of managers at all levels, beginning with senior leadership, who set the business strategy down through the entire organization. This often involves changing specific aspects of the existing culture since achieving optimal levels of work-life effectiveness requires tight alignment of shared values.

- Performance planning is a process whereby expectations are established linking an individual with team and organizational goals. Care is taken to ensure goals at all levels are aligned and there is a clear line of sight from performance expectations of individual employees all the way up to organizational objectives and strategies set at the highest levels of the organization.
- Performance is the manner of demonstrating a skill or capacity.
- Performance feedback communicates how well people do a job or task compared to expectations, performance standards and goals. Performance feedback can motivate employees to improve performance.

Recognition can also play a vital role in employee engagement. Recognition should accomplish the following:

- Reinforce the value of performance improvement.
- Foster continued improvement, although it is not guaranteed.
- Formalize the process of showing appreciation.
- Provide positive and immediate feedback.
- Foster communication of valued behavior and activities.

Development and career opportunities are defined as follows:

- Development comprises learning experiences designed to enhance employees' skills and competencies.
- Career opportunities involve plans to help employees pursue their career goals.

Development and career opportunities include the following:

- Learning opportunities
  - Tuition assistance
  - Corporate universities
  - New technology training
  - Attendance at outside seminars, conferences, virtual education, etc.
  - Self-development tools and techniques
  - On-the-job learning; rotational assignments at a progressively higher level
  - Sabbaticals with the express purpose of acquiring specific skills, knowledge or experience.
- Coaching/Mentoring
  - Leadership training
  - Access to experts/information networks
  - Exposure to resident experts
  - Formal (or informal) mentoring programs, in or outside one's organization.

- Advancement opportunities
  - Internships
  - Apprenticeships with experts
  - Overseas assignments
  - Internal job postings
  - Job advancement/promotion
  - Career ladders and pathways
  - Succession planning
  - Defined and respectable "on and off ramps" throughout the career life cycle.

As noted earlier, the components of the total rewards model overlap, interact, integrate and work synergistically with each other. The total rewards model helps drive value proposition factors for the employee and employer. By allowing the total rewards proposition to bend and flex, organizations will be able to utilize components to attract, motivate and retain.

While there are common influences for all businesses within certain sectors of the economy, each organization has unique circumstances that will influence its total rewards decisions. This is the organization's point of strategic advantage.

The total rewards model can have a very different look and feel based upon specific organizational values and needs. In the WorldatWork core model, each component can play a bigger or smaller role in the entire package and can relate to the other components in differing ways. What makes the integration of these specific elements challenging is that employee needs and values differ within organizations. These value differences are typically based upon their life experiences and current life needs, and determine their sense of what the total rewards package should look like.

Legal and Regulatory Environments 2

Compensation programs have been significantly influenced by federal, state and local legislation and regulation in the last 70 years. To effectively develop and manage compensation programs within legal constraints, an understanding of the provisions and limitations of applicable laws and regulations is necessary. This section describes federal legislation that significantly impacts pay program administration. It is important to note that some states have laws that are more favorable to the employee than the federal law. In these instances, the state law will trump the federal law. (For example, in California, overtime is paid to employees after working eight hours in one day, versus the federal law that requires overtime after 40 hours in a single work week.)

Prior to 1930, legislative action on compensation arrangements between employers and workers was looked upon with suspicion; courts and labor unions were skeptical of such intervention. However, the length and severity of the "Great Depression" made economic security a higher priority, and government action came to be regarded as necessary.

Sherman Anti-Trust Act

The Sherman Anti-Trust Act of 1890, although initially not intended for compensation-type issues, affects almost all compensation practitioners. The Sherman Anti-Trust Act has its roots in the early industrialization of the United States, when companies that established an industry could monopolize it and eliminate potential competition. This act, as it relates to compensation, has been applied in situations where organizations have engaged in "price fixing" of wages. The argument has been made that employers have fixed the price of wages through open disclosure of information in salary surveys and projections of budget increases. In fact, throughout the last few decades, several cases have gone to court regarding price fixing of wages — Federal Reserve Bank of Boston, Utah Health Care Group and Exxon. With the Utah healthcare association, the courts created a consent decree regarding how that group can utilize compensation data. Although this decree only applies in that situation, most survey vendors and organizations have adopted guidelines from the consent decree when conducting surveys. The consent decree listed the following guidelines to ensure that the survey data is not in violation of the act:

- The data must be at least three months old. Most survey vendors wait at least three months after collecting the data to report the data (which helps fulfill this requirement).

- There needs to be a minimum of five organizations matching a given job. By requiring at least five organizations, it will be difficult for any one organization's anonymity to be breached.
- No one organization should represent more than 25 percent of the incumbents for a given job match. By minimizing the effect of one organization in a survey, the results are less likely to be skewed by a single company's pay practice.

Davis-Bacon Act

The earliest recorded effort to enlarge federal economic control was the passage of the Davis-Bacon Act in 1931. Under this act, the Department of Labor is authorized to establish, by locality, wage-payment schedules to be used by all bidders seeking construction contracts with the federal government in excess of $2,000. Employees of such construction contractors must be paid the special federal "prevailing" wages and fringe benefits established by the Secretary of Labor. Pay is typically interpreted by the government as union-equivalent wages and benefits in the construction trade positions.

National Labor Relations Act

The National Labor Relations Act (NLRA) of 1935 was enacted with the intention of creating a better environment for collective bargaining. The NLRA was created to provide a more equitable environment for labor- and management-dispute resolution, and covers all employers involved in interstate commerce (with the exception of airlines, railroads, agriculture and the government). The NLRA guarantees the right of employees to select or reject third-party representation, as well as the rules for bargaining in good faith and controlling against unfair labor practices. The enforcing agency of the NLRA is the National Labor Relations Board (NLRB). It is interesting to note that neither the federal courts nor the U.S. Department of Labor have jurisdiction in matters concerning the NLRB.

Walsh-Healey Act

The Walsh-Healey Act, passed in 1936, provided general employment regulations for employers holding manufacturing or supply contracts with the federal government in excess of $10,000. While originally requiring payment of overtime rates (time-and-one-half) for hours worked in excess of eight per day or 40 per week, the law was amended in 1986 to eliminate the requirement to pay overtime rates after eight hours in a workday. Although the law requires employees to be paid the minimum prevailing manufacturing wage established by the Secretary of Labor, the secretary has, as a result of litigation, issued the minimum wage as the "prevailing" wage since the 1960s. The law also established certain child labor and safety standards. The U.S. Department of Labor (DOL) is the enforcing agency for the Walsh-Healey Act.

Fair Labor Standards Act

The federal legislation that most significantly affects the design of direct compensation (cash) programs is the Fair Labor Standards Act (FLSA) of 1938. Much of the terminology used by compensation professionals is traceable to the provisions of the act, and its influence is clearly evident in the pay programs of employers covered by the act.

Employers engaged in interstate or foreign commerce have been covered since the law was passed in 1938, and numerous other employers were included in later amendments to the act. It always has been interpreted very broadly, to include practically any employer of any size.

The FLSA's primary objective was to eliminate working conditions that were detrimental to the health and well being of workers. This was accomplished by the establishment of minimum wage, overtime pay, recordkeeping and child labor standards for all covered establishments unless a specific exemption is applied.

Minimum Wage

The federal minimum wage was established by FLSA at 25 cents per hour. By 1981, it had been raised to $3.35 an hour and in 1997 it was raised to $5.15 per hour. (The act provides for changes in the minimum wage through federal legislation). Additionally, for tipped positions, the minimum wage is $3.15 per hour, as long as the employee's tips raise the hourly rate to at least federal minimum wage, or $5.15 per hour.

Overtime Pay

The FLSA requires all nonexempt employees be paid at least one-and-one-half times their regular hourly rate of pay for hours worked in excess of 40 in a workweek (or, in certain special cases, for hours exceeding eight in any one day or 80 in a two-week period). The workweek generally is defined as seven consecutive 24-hour periods, which may start at any time and may be different for various employee groups. Because overtime must be calculated on a weekly basis, overtime worked in one week may not be balanced against straight-time hours not worked in another week, unless special exceptions exist in the law.

"Hours worked" include the time an employee is required to be on duty or on the employer's premises, or at other prescribed places of work, and any other time that he or she is "permitted or suffered" to work for the employer. "Hours worked" can include time spent in training programs, travel time within the workday, sleeping time if the tour of duty is less than 24 hours, a rest period of less than 20 minutes, changing (clothes) time, waiting time and work performed at home.

The regulation specifically addresses the issue of comp time (paid time off) in lieu of overtime. This practice is acceptable in the public sector, but is considered illegal in the private sector. Cash is the extra compensation for overtime, not time off.

In addition to the base rate, any bonus that the employee may receive could factor into the overtime calculation. Bonus payments can be defined as any payments that are in addition to the regular earnings of an employee. This is determined by the period the bonus covers and the type of bonus. The DOL discusses seven specified types of payments that would be excluded from the regular rate, and therefore excluded from being included in an overtime calculation.

- Discretionary bonuses
- Gifts
- Payments in the nature of gifts on special occasions
- Contributions by the employer to certain welfare plans
- Payments made by the employer pursuant to certain profit-sharing plans
- Payments made by the employer pursuant to certain thrift plans
- Payments made by the employer pursuant to certain savings plans.

Bonuses which do not qualify for exclusion from the regular rate as one of these types must be totaled in with other earnings to determine the regular rate on which overtime pay must be based.

For an organization to include the bonus payment into the regular rate of pay, the organization needs to determine which pay period(s) the bonus is related to. The DOL separates the recalculation of overtime into four categories: (1) when the bonus covers only one weekly pay period, (2) when the bonus covers several weekly pay periods, (3) when the bonus cannot be identified with particular workweeks (workweek example) and (4) when the bonus cannot be identified with particular workweeks (hourly example).

In the first case (when a bonus covers only one weekly pay period), the additional overtime is simple to calculate. The employer would add the bonus amount to the weekly earnings and divide by the total number of hours worked. This calculation will give the employer the new regular rate for overtime purposes.

Example: You have a call-center employee who worked 45 hours during the workweek. Because that employee had achieved all of the required times, he receives a $100 weekly bonus. The employee's wages are $10/hour or $400/week. To calculate the new rate for overtime you would take the weekly wage of $450 (45 hours X $10) and add the $100 bonus amount to get $550. To calculate the new regular rate you would divide $550 by 45 (hours worked) to get the new hourly wage of $12.22. So the additional amount you would need to include for overtime purposes would be $30.55 ($12.22 X 5 [hours of overtime] X .50 [overtime factor]). So for the week, the employee would receive a paycheck for $580.55 ($450 [$10/hour X 45 hours] + $30.55 [overtime amount due to the bonus] + $100 [bonus]).

For the second situation, the same process will be used, however, the bonus would be distributed over several pay periods. The regulation states the following formula: "When the amount of the bonus can be ascertained, it must be apportioned back over the workweeks of the period during which it may be said to have been earned. The employee must then receive an additional amount of compensation for each workweek that he worked overtime during the period equal to one-half of the hourly rate of pay allocable to the bonus for that week multiplied by the number of statutory overtime hours worked during the week."

Example: You have an administrative assistant who earns a performance bonus for the month of February. The month of February had four weeks, and the administrative assistant worked the following hours: 40, 42, 40 and 43. She receives a performance bonus of $200. To find the additional amount required for overtime, you would take the total amount of the bonus ($200) and divide by total hours worked (165 hours) to get the bonus hourly rate of $1.21/hour. According to the regulation, you would then multiply .5 (one half) by the bonus hourly rate ($1.21) by the number of overtime hours (5) to have an additional payment due of $3.03 (.5 X $1.21 X 5).

For the third situation, the DOL states, "it may be reasonable and equitable to assume that the employee earned an equal amount of bonus each week of the period to which the bonus relates, and if the facts support this assumption additional compensation for each overtime week of the period may be computed and paid in an amount equal to one-half of the average hourly increase in pay resulting from bonus allocated to the week, multiplied by the number of statutory overtime hours worked in that week." Basically, the regulation is stating that you can assume the employee earned an equal amount of bonus for each week he was eligible, very similar to situation No. 2 above.

Example: You have a front-line supervisor who earns a performance bonus based on an increase of widgets produced, for a six-month period. The supervisor earns $15/hour and worked about 52 hours overtime during the six-month period. The performance bonus was $1,000.

To calculate the additional overtime amount, you would take the amount of the bonus ($1,000) divided by the number of weeks the bonus was allotted (26 weeks) to get $38.46/week. That would mean the average hourly increase would be the additional weekly amount ($38.46) divided by the number of hours worked each week (for this example, we will assume the supervisor worked two overtime hours each week for a total of 42 hours/week) to get an average hourly increase of $0.92. According to the formula above, you would then multiply the hourly rate ($0.92) by the overtime factor (.5) by the number of overtime hours (52) to have an additional payment due of $23.92 (.5 X $0.92 X 52).

The fourth situation the DOL discusses is when it may not be feasible to assign an equal bonus to each workweek. The DOL states, "it may be reasonable and equitable to assume that the employee earned an equal amount of bonus each hour of the pay period and the resultant hourly increase may be determined by dividing the total bonus by the number of hours worked by the employee during the period for which it is paid. The additional compensation due for the overtime workweeks in the period may then be computed by multiplying the total number of statutory overtime hours worked in each such workweek during the period by one-half this hourly increase."

Example: You have a retail store assistant manager who earns an annual bonus based on profit. The assistant manager earns $17/hour and worked a total of 2,340 hours (260 overtime) for the year. The bonus was $2,500.

For this example, you would take the total bonus amount ($2,500) and divide by the total number of hours worked (2,340) for an additional overtime amount of $1.07/hour. You would then multiply the amount ($1.07) by the overtime factor (.5) by the number of overtime hours (260) to have an additional payment due of $139.10 ($1.07 X .5 X 260).

Occasionally, a bonus may be written as a percent of the employee's wages. If the plan is written so the bonus would include a percentage of both straight time and overtime, you would not need to recalculate the overtime. The example in the regulation is a performance bonus that pays 10 percent of straight time and 10 percent of overtime earnings. Take note, the regulation states this is an acceptable practice, as long as it is not used to circumvent the overtime requirements of the act.

According to the regulation, employers would not need to factor in overtime for a true discretionary bonus. The DOL describes a discretionary bonus as follows:

- The fact that payment is to be made is determined at the sole discretion of the employer
- The amount of payment to be made is determined at the sole discretion of the employer.
- Both the above situations are not pursuant to any prior contract, agreement or promise causing the employee to expect such payments regularly.

The regulation has examples of situations in which the bonus is not discretionary:

- If an employer promises in advance to pay a bonus, he has abandoned his discretion with regard to it.
- If an employer promises to pay their sales employees one cent for each item sold, this payment is discretionary depending on the financial condition of the firm. The amount of the bonus is no longer discretionary, but the payment is.

For gifts, money paid at Christmas or special occasions, these bonuses may be excluded from the regular rate, and therefore excluded from the overtime recalculation. To qualify for this exclusion, the bonus must actually be a gift or in the nature of a gift. It cannot be measured by hours worked, production or efficiency. If the payment is geared toward wages and hours worked, production or efficiency, then it is no longer considered a gift and must be included in the regular rate for overtime purposes.

The DOL has several regulations pertaining to circumventing the overtime recalculations. This is one of those regulations. This regulation pertains to when an employer designates a portion of regular wages as a bonus. The employer is not allowed to pursue this practice and the DOL will take action if this practice occurs.

An illustration of how this type of plan works over a three-week period may serve to illustrate this principle more clearly:
1. You have an employee who earns $400/week without regard to the number of hours worked
2. In the first week, the employee whose applicable maximum hours standard is 40 hours works 40 hours and receives $400. The books show he has received $206 (40 hours X $5.15/hour) as wages and $194 as bonus. No overtime has been worked, so no overtime compensation is due.
3. In the second week, he works 45 hours and receives $400. The books show he has received $206 for the first 40 hours and $38.63 (5 hours X $7.73 an hour) for the five hours over 40, or a total of $244.63 as wages, and the balance as a bonus of $155.38. The employer then computes overtime compensation by dividing $155.38 by 45 hours to discover the average hourly increase resulting from the bonus — $3.45/hour — and half this rate is paid for the five overtime hours—$8.43. This is wrong. The employee's regular rate in this week is $8.89 ($400 divided by 45 hours). Therefore he is owed $422.28 [($8.89 X 40hours) + ($8.89 X 1.5 X 5 hours)], not $408.43.
4. In the third week, the employee works 50 hours and is paid $400. The books show the employee received $206 for the first 40 hours and $115.95 (10 hours X $7.73 an hour) for the 10 hours over 40, for a total of $321.95, and the balance as a bonus of $78.05. Overtime pay due on the "bonus" is found to be $7.81. This is wrong. The employee's regular rate in the week is $8. Therefore $440 is owed, not $407.81.

Exemption

Exempted from the overtime pay and minimum wage provisions of the act are executives, professionals, administrators, computer professionals and outside sales staff. The act also provides for other specific exemptions. For employees to be exempt from the statutes for the FLSA, they must pass three tests — salary basis, salary level and duties. It is important to note that classification of exempt or nonexempt by using a job title alone will not determine if that position is exempt. The employer needs to be cognizant of the employee's job duties to ensure that the employee's duties fall within the range of the regulations. It is also extremely important to ensure the job descriptions are accurate and up-to-date, and that all job specifications listed on the description are being performed by the employee.

Example: Company A could have an executive assistant to the CEO exercising independent judgment with respect to matters of significance and performing executive assistant duties which would classify her as exempt. Yet in Company B an executive assistant might type memos, schedule appointments and perform duties that are not defined as exempt, and hence, the job is classified as nonexempt. It is even feasible that two people in Company A who have the title of executive assistant have differing duties, and one could be exempt while the other could be nonexempt.

Salary Basis

To be considered salaried under the FLSA exemption means to be paid the full salary for the workweek regardless of the number of hours worked, the quality of work or the quantity of work during that workweek.

Salary Limit

An employee must pass the salary limit test to be considered exempt. The salary limit test is the same for all exemption categories (except outside sales), and is $455 per week. This $455 per week equates to $23,660 a year. Any employee earning less than $455 per week ($23,660 a year) in base salary will be classified as a nonexempt employee, regardless of the duties performed. The salary limit is effective for all of the United States and its territories, except American Samoa. For employees in American Samoa the lower limit is $380/week.

In addition to the lower limit of $455 per week, the DOL recognized that occasionally an employer has an employee that earns more than $100,000 per year, yet does not meet the exemption requirements, therefore is a nonexempt employee. The DOL has established a "bright line exemption" for employees who do not meet the all of the primary-duty requirements for the exemption tests, yet could still be considered exempt. The DOL has determined that any employee earning more than $100,000 per year who meets one of the primary-duties requirements (executive, administrative, professional), performing office/nonmanual work, yet is not considered exempt can be exempt from overtime. This $100,000-per-year salary must include at least $455 per week in base salary, however the remaining amount would be considered "total annual compensation." Total annual compensation can include commissions, nondiscretionary bonus and other nondiscretionary compensation. Total annual compensation does not include benefits (for example, 401(k) contributions, payment for medical insurance).

Duties Tests

Each of the six classifications of exempt employees has its own duties tests (executive, administrative, learned professional, creative professional, computer professional and outside sales).

The first duties test covered is the executive test. If the employee meets the salary-basis and the salary-level test, the following are the duties the executive needs to perform to be an exempt employee:
- Has the primary duty of managing the enterprise or a recognized department or subdivision

- Customarily and regularly directs the work of two or more other full-time employees (or their equivalent)
- Has the authority to hire or fire other employees (or recommend the hiring, firing, advancement, promotion or any other change of status of other employees).

The second exemption is the administrative exemption:

- Has the primary duty of performing office or nonmanual work directly related to the management or general business operations of the employer or the employer's customers
- Exercises discretion and independent judgment with respect to matters of significance.

A third exemption is the learned professional:

- Has the primary duty of performing work requiring advanced knowledge, defined as work that is predominantly intellectual in character and that includes work requiring the consistent exercise of discretion and judgment
- Has advanced knowledge in a field of science or learning
- Has advanced knowledge customarily acquired by a prolonged course of specialized intellectual instruction.

The fourth exemption is the creative professional:

- Has the primary duty of the performance of work requiring invention, imagination, originality or talent in a recognized field of artistic endeavor.

The final two exemptions are a little different then the first four. The computer professional, in addition to the salary requirements, allows for the employee to earn an hourly wage and still be exempt. The hourly wage is $27.63 per hour. For the computer professional, the following is the duties test:

- Employed as a computer systems analyst, computer programmer, software engineer or other similarly skilled worker in the computer field performing the following duties:
  - (A) application of systems analysis techniques and procedures, including consulting with users to determine hardware, software or system-functional applications
  - (B) design, development, documentation, analysis, creation, testing or modification of computer systems or programs, including prototypes, based on and related to user or system-design specifications
  - (C) design, documentation, testing, creation or modification of computer programs related to machine operating systems
  - (D) a combination of duties described in (A), (B) and (C), the performance of which requires the same level of skills.

The outside sales exemption has no set salary requirement and consists of the following duties:

- Has the primary duty of making sales (any sale, exchange contract to sell, consignment for sales, shipment for sale or other disposition; includes the transfer of title to tangible property, and in certain cases, of tangible and valuable evidences of intangible property), or obtaining orders or contracts for services or for the use of facilities for which a consideration will be paid by the client or customer
- Must be customarily and regularly engaged away from the employer's place or places of business.

Child Labor Provisions

Restrictions on child labor are designed to protect the educational opportunities of minors, as well as their health and well-being. Fourteen is the minimum age for virtually all nonagricultural work covered by the act. Sixteen is the minimum age for employment in a nonagricultural occupation that is declared nonhazardous by the secretary of labor. Eighteen is the age at which there is no restriction on the type of work that may be performed.

The following FLSA provisions apply to the employment of children 14 to 16 years of age and provide rules for the periods and conditions of employment:

- Work must be outside of school hours.
- The child may not work more than 40 hours in any one week when school is not in session and no more than 18 hours a week when school is in session.
- The child may not work more than eight hours in any one day when school is not in session and no more than three hours when school is in session.
- The child may work only between the hours of 7 a.m. and 7 p.m. in any one day except during the summer when the evening hour will be extended to 9 p.m.
- There is a special exemption for minors age 14 and 15 who are employed to perform sports-attending services at professional sporting events

Children 14 to 18 years old are banned from the following occupations considered to be hazardous:

- Occupations in or about plants or establishments manufacturing or storing explosives or articles containing explosive components
- Coal-mine occupations
- Logging operations; occupations in the operation of any saw, lathe, or shingle; or cooperage stock mills
- Occupations involved in the operation of power-driven woodworking machines
- Occupations with exposure to radioactive substances and to ionizing radiations
- Occupations in the operation of power-driven meat-processing machines
- Occupations involved in the operation of bakery machines

- Occupations involved in the manufacture of brick, tile and kindred products
- Occupations in roofing operations.

Recordkeeping

Employers are required to keep individual employee records on wages, hours and certain other information. These records must be saved for at least three years. No particular form is required with regard to exempt employees, but the following records must be maintained for nonexempt employees:

- Name and home address
- Birth date if the employee is younger than 19 years of age
- Sex and occupation
- Hour and day when the workweek begins for the employee
- Regular hourly pay rate for any week when overtime is worked
- Hours worked each workday and total hours worked each workweek
- Total daily or weekly straight-time earnings
- Total overtime pay for the work week
- Deductions from or additions to wages, and total wages paid each pay period
- Date of payment and pay period covered.

FLSA Enforcement

The Wage and Hour Division of the U.S. Department of Labor is responsible for enforcing the FLSA. Authorized representatives may investigate and gather data regarding wages, hours and other conditions and practices of employment, and may enter establishments to inspect the premises, review and transcribe records and interview employees.

A two-year statute of limitations applies to recovery of back wages except in the case of willful violations, for which there is a three-year statute of limitations. Willful violations also may be prosecuted criminally and the violator fined. A second conviction may result in imprisonment.

Service Contract Act

Passed in 1965, the Service Contract Act applies to federal contracts for services in excess of $2,500 and requires service contractors to pay minimum wages and fringe benefits as established to be prevailing by the Secretary of Labor. As with the Davis-Bacon Act, pay scales are based upon "prevailing" wages, which is typically interpreted by the government as union-equivalent wages and benefits in the local labor market. The act also includes certain safety standards. The U.S. Department of Labor is the enforcing agency of the Service Contract Act.

Recordkeeping and posting requirements, government investigations and hearings, court actions and blacklisting of violators have been established as enforcement mechanisms for the Davis-Bacon, Walsh-Healey and Service Contract Acts.

Anti-Discrimination Laws

The federal government enacted a number of statutes in the 1960s that were designed to ensure the fair treatment of specific segments of the population in regard to their rights as individuals and employees. The most important of these are the Equal Pay Act of 1963 and Title VII of the Civil Rights Act of 1964.

Equal Pay Act

As early as World War II, the National War Labor Board was created as the arbiter of salary disputes between labor and management. In 1942, it issued an order for salary adjustments to "equalize the wage or salary rates paid to females with rates paid to males for comparable quality and quantity of work on the same or similar operations." A bill requiring "equal pay for comparable work" performed by males and females was introduced in Congress in 1945 and rejected, as were several similar bills for the next 18 years.

The Equal Pay Act, which prohibits gender-based compensation discrimination, was successfully enacted in 1963. Specifically, the act prohibits an employer from discriminating "between employees on the basis of sex by paying wages to employees ... at a rate less than the rate at which he pays wage to employees of the opposite sex ... for equal work on jobs that require equal skill, effort and responsibility, and are performed under similar working conditions ...." There are, however, four exceptions (affirmative defenses). Unequal payments can be based on (1) a seniority system, (2) a merit system, (3) a system which measures quantity or quality of production or (4) any other factor aside from gender.

The act, an amendment to the Fair Labor Standards Act, was originally enforced by the Wage and Hour Division of the Department of Labor, and employers subject to the FLSA were subject to the provisions of the Equal Pay Act as well. In 1979, the Equal Employment Opportunity Commission (EEOC) became the enforcing agency.

Plaintiffs who file lawsuits under the Equal Pay Act must show that they are paid less than a person of the opposite sex for doing substantially equal work (in the same job family) which requires substantially equal skill, effort and responsibility and is performed under similar working conditions. Once the *prima facie* case has been established, the burden shifts to the employer to prove that the pay difference is based upon a seniority system, a merit system, a system that measures earnings by quantity or quality of production or some other factor aside from gender.

The "bottom line" of the Equal Pay Act for pay-program design and administration is that if, on the average, men and women are paid different rates when they perform work that is substantially the same, these differences must be shown to be attributable to one of the "allowable differences."

The effects of the Equal Pay Act have been far-reaching and include the revision of employee benefits programs to eliminate gender-based differentials; greater emphasis on written job descriptions; greater emphasis on job-content-oriented procedures for assignment of pay grades and ranges to specific jobs; and greater emphasis on written policies and procedures.

Title VII of the Civil Rights Act

The most comprehensive of the civil rights statutes, this legislation was created to prohibit discrimination by employers on the basis of race, color, religion, gender or national origin, in the hiring, firing, training, compensation or promotion of employees. On the last day of debate, gender was added as a prohibited basis of discrimination, creating overlap with the Equal Pay Act.

For cases subject to this overlap on sex-discrimination in pay, the Senate added the Bennett Amendment, which (ambiguously) states, "It shall not be an unlawful employment practice under Title VII for any employer to differentiate upon the basis of sex in determining the amount of the wages or compensation paid to employees of such employer if such differentiation is authorized by the provisions of the Equal Pay Act." Regardless of how the amendment is interpreted, differences in pay may be defended if attributable to work that is not substantially equal, or is based on seniority merit or quantity and quality of work.

The Civil Rights Act is enforced by the EEOC, which was created by the act. Virtually all employers with 15 or more employees are covered.

Employees who file lawsuits under the act must demonstrate either "disparate treatment" or "disparate impact." Under "disparate treatment," the plaintiff must prove that the employer deliberately discriminated, based on the employee's race, color, religion, national origin or gender. If this is done, the employer must demonstrate a legitimate nondiscriminatory basis to justify the practice. Then, in order to prevail, the employee must prove that any such "justification" is just a pretext for discrimination.

Under "disparate impact," the employee must establish a *prima facie* case showing adverse impact on a protected class. Then the employer must validate the challenged practice by demonstrating a business necessity for the practice and proving that no alternative exists that would produce a less adverse impact.

The bottom line of Title VII for pay-program design and administration is that pay programs should produce pay rates that treat all classes of employees similarly, and any differences should be attributable to job-related, defensible causes (seniority, performance and the like). Case law resulting from litigation under Title VII created the concept of "bona fide occupational qualifications"

(BFOQ). This concept specifies that job qualifications imposed by employers must be defensible and necessary in order for an employee to perform the job.

Age Discrimination in Employment Act

The Age Discrimination in Employment Act, passed in 1967 and amended in 1978 and 1986, protects workers aged 40 and older from employment discrimination. While it prohibits discrimination in all terms and conditions of employment, it has been applied principally in cases involving retirement, promotions and layoff policies.

The purpose of the act is to "promote employment of older persons based on their ability rather than age, to prohibit arbitrary age discrimination in employment, and to help employers and workers find ways of solving problems arising from the impact of age on employment."

The law prohibits mandatory retirement (with some exceptions, generally involving public safety); limiting or classifying employees in any way related to their age (such as with maturity curves); reducing any employee's wage in order to comply with the act; and indicating any preference based on age in notices of employment. Individual state laws sometimes are more restrictive than the federal law.

The act applies to employers of 20 or more persons, as well as to federal, state and local governments. Employment agencies serving covered employers and labor unions with 25 or more members are also included under the provisions of the act.

There are several statutory exceptions to the ADEA:

- Bona fide executives who are entitled to $44,000 per year or more in retirement benefits from employer contributions; also, there is a mandatory retirement age of 65 that is allowed
- Elected (or high-level appointed) officials in the government
- Bona Fide Occupational Qualifications (BFOQ), which can be defined as an occupational qualification that is reasonably necessary to the normal operation of the employer's business; employers may discriminate on the basis of age if it is reasonably necessary.
- Seniority systems.

The EEOC has been charged with the enforcement of the act since July 1979. The plaintiff must prove that he or she is a member of a protected group and that he or she has been adversely affected by a personnel policy or action (*prima facie* case). Once this is established, the burden shifts to the employer, who may argue that the adverse treatment occurred on the basis of considerations other than age or that the decision or policy was *rightly* based on age (for example, if age is a BFOQ for the job).

Executive Order 11246

This presidential order, signed by President Johnson in 1965, requires companies holding federal contracts or subcontracts in excess of $10,000 not to discriminate in their employment practices (which include pay practices) on the basis of race, gender, religion or national origin, and to take affirmative action to ensure that their employment decisions are made in a nondiscriminatory manner. For service and supply contracts in excess of $50,000, contractors must also develop and implement written affirmative action plans which include goals and objectives of increasing minority and female participation in their workforce.

The executive order is enforced by the Office of Federal Contract Compliance Programs (OFCCP) in the U.S. Department of Labor, which investigates complaints of discrimination and also conducts on-site compliance reviews to determine federal contractors' compliance with the executive order mandates.

Vocation Rehabilitation Act of 1973

The act covers persons employed by, or seeking employment from, federal departments and agencies or businesses performing federal contract work in excess of $2,500. Recipients of federal assistance are also protected from discrimination based on any mental or physical disability that substantially limits one or more major life activities. Section 503 of the act applies to private industry and Section 504 applies to institutions receiving federal grants. Discrimination in employment is prohibited in all terms and conditions of employment, which certainly includes compensation.

The act is enforced by the OFCCP, which requires covered employers to utilize affirmative action to employ and advance qualified handicapped individuals. The act also requires employers "to make reasonable accommodation to the known physical or mental limitations of an otherwise qualified, handicapped applicant, employee or participant." Further, the act requires the elimination of physical barriers, to ensure that the "facility is readily accessible to and usable by qualified handicapped individuals."

Charges under the act proceed in exactly the same way as Title VII. If, for example, a human-capital policy or action has an adverse effect on a handicapped person, the employer must then show that the adverse treatment was based on considerations other than the handicap (for example, seniority or performance), or that the handicap was a legitimate basis for such policy or action. This last defense is rare in compensation cases.

Vietnam Era Veterans Readjustment Act of 1974

The Vietnam Era Veterans Readjustment Act requires companies holding federal contracts or subcontracts of $10,000 or more to take affirmative action and not to discriminate in the employment and advancement in employment of qualified, special disabled veterans and veterans of the Vietnam era.

The act is also enforced by the OFCCP, which investigates complaints and checks for compliance with the act during on-site investigations.

Americans with Disabilities Act

The Americans with Disabilities Act (ADA) of 1990 was enacted to include any company involved in interstate commerce with 15 or more employees. The act is enforced by the EEOC and dictates that the charge of discrimination must by filed within180 days of the alleged discriminatory act.

A disability can be defined as an impairment that substantially limits or restricts a major life activity such as hearing, seeing, speaking, breathing, performing manual tasks, walking, caring for oneself, learning or working. Any employee or job applicant who meets the following criteria may be covered under the ADA:

- Has a physical or mental impairment that substantially limits one or more of the major life activities
- Has a record of any such impairments
- Is regarded as having such impairments
- Is associated with anyone having such impairments

This provision is designed to protect any qualified individual, whether or not he is disabled, from disability-related discrimination.

It is important to note that the individual must be qualified for the job and must be able to perform the essential functions of the job. Essential functions can be defined as those functions that include the following criteria:

- Reason the position exists is to perform the function
- Limited number of other employees available to perform the function
- Degree of expertise or skill required to perform the function.

Under the ADA, if an employer can reasonably accommodate a request by a disabled employee (or applicant), it is required to accept it. A reasonable accommodation is any change or adjustment to a job or work environment that permits a qualified applicant or employee with a disability to participate in the job-application process, to perform the essential functions of a job or to enjoy benefits and privileges of employment equal to those enjoyed by employees without disabilities. It is a violation of the ADA to fail to provide reasonable accommodation to the known physical or mental limitations of a qualified individual with a disability, unless to do so would impose an undue hardship on the operation of the business. Undue hardship means the accommodation would require significant difficulty or expense. The act specifies three criteria to measure reasonableness of accommodations:

- Size of the business
- Number (or type) of facilities
  - Budgetary constraints
  - Type of operation
  - The composition
  - The makeup of the workplace
- Nature and cost of accommodations.

The Job Process   3

Pay structures are the foundation of most employee compensation programs; they are job hierarchies with pay rates and/or pay ranges assigned. Implicit in the construction and use of pay structures is the premise that the greater the worth of a job — as determined by job content and labor-market analysis — the higher its pay grade and range.

Thus, regardless of the methodology selected for their development, pay grades and ranges ultimately are determined by the following:

- Market rates for comparable jobs in other organizations — *external* competitiveness
- Management's judgment as to the relative internal worth of the job's content — *internal* equity.

Organizations may emphasize either external competitiveness or internal equity, but they will blend and balance the two to meet their overall employee-relations objectives.

The process of developing a pay structure involves a series of steps. These steps include the following:

- Job analysis
- Job documentation
- Job evaluation — for example, development of the job-worth hierarchy using
  - Market pricing
  - Job content
- Establishment of pay rates or ranges — for example, the base pay structure. (See Figure 3-1 on page 32.)

The first two steps toward building and maintaining a pay structure — job analysis and documentation — typically involve systematic approaches to job content definition and written job descriptions (or some other form of written job documentation). Defensibility and decision-making in compensation programs are enhanced through effective application of these two steps, and their role in developing pay rates for jobs becomes more important as organization size and complexity increase.

Job Analysis

Job analysis, simply defined, is collecting and evaluating relevant information about jobs. The first step in the job analysis process is to determine specifically what information is to be collected. The data collected should clarify the *nature* of work

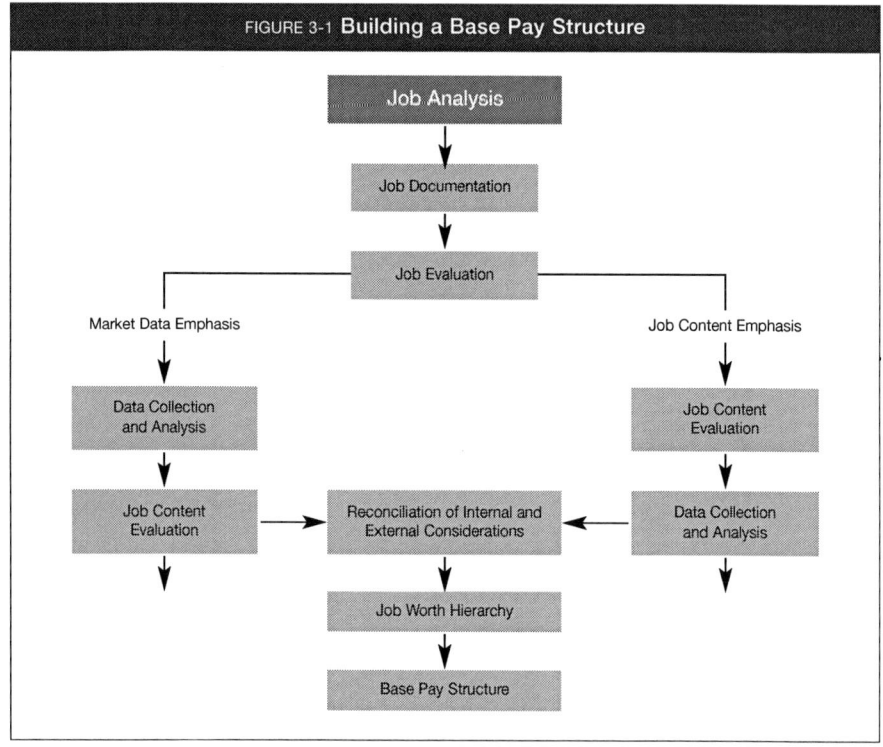

FIGURE 3-1 **Building a Base Pay Structure**

being performed (including principal tasks, duties and responsibilities) as well as the level of work being performed. Data should include the extent and types of knowledge, skill, mental and physical effort, and responsibility required for the work being performed. Reviewing the minimal job requirements for knowledge, skill, mental and physical effort will allow the organization to have a written documentation for ADA purposes. Work environment, hazards and general physical conditions, which affect the work, also may be pertinent.

In collecting information about jobs, there are primary data sources and secondary data sources:

A. *Primary* data sources are employees who are actually performing or supervising the work. There are four commonly used techniques for collecting job information from primary sources:
   1. Questionnaires — can be defined as a written set of questions regarding job content that requires the incumbent to either:
      a. Prepare a narrative response (open-ended)
      b. Provide limited responses to a predetermined set of answers (highly structured)
      c. Advantages:
         i. Flexibility; can be created/tailored to the job group being analyzed

ii. Consistency; everyone will be answering the same set of questions
   iii. Can cover a large number of jobs
  d. Disadvantages:
   i. Follow-up questions (open-ended) may be required if the questions/responses are not clearly defined/answered.
   ii. Questions can be time consuming and expensive to develop and to complete.
   iii. Questions (and responses for highly structured questions) need to be validated first.
   iv. If the questionnaire is too long, the employees may grow tired of answering the questions and the data will be incomplete and/or inaccurate.
2. Interviews — can be defined as follows:
  a. Structured, one-on-one review of job content by a job analyst and an incumbent or supervisor (individual)
  b. A structured review of job content between a job analyst and a group of incumbents (group)
  c. Advantages:
   i. The job description is created based upon direct information from the person (or group) being interviewed.
   ii. Interviews allow buy-in into the process, because the participants will feel they are directly influencing the results.
   iii. When using group interviews, the results will have greater validity due to several sources.
  d. Disadvantages:
   i. Interviews can be costly in time and resources.
   ii. In a group interview, a dominant participant might sidetrack the conversation, as well as cause other participants not to participate.
3. Logs or diaries — can be defined as a written account of tasks the incumbent completes while working
  a. Advantages:
   i. Accurate descriptions because the incumbent records information while they complete the tasks
   ii. Multiple sources can be used
  b. Disadvantages:
   i. Incumbent might not record every task completed
   ii. Potential for embellishing tasks.

4. Direct Observation — can be defined as:
   a. Observing workers to understand:
      i. Job Duties
      ii. Responsibilities
      iii. Tasks
   b. Advantages:
      i. For short-cycle work, observations can be done fairly easily to identify which tasks are being completed and to confirm behaviors.
   c. Disadvantages:
      i. Can be a time-consuming and costly process in terms of resources used (time requirement to observe employees doing their job)
      ii. May not be sufficient information to determine job specifications — for example, the skills, abilities and behaviors necessary for successful performance of the job
      iii. Not as useful in higher level jobs.

As you can see, each of these techniques has advantages and disadvantages; the organization should weigh the costs, the complexity and the availability of resources to determine which approach will achieve the best results. Most compensation plans use more than one method of acquiring data from primary sources, striving for comprehensiveness, accuracy, flexibility, administrative efficiency and uniformity.

B. All other sources of information about jobs are referred to as *secondary* sources. Some frequently used secondary sources of information about jobs include the Bureau of Labor Statistics O*NET and the Occupational Outlook Handbook; pay surveys; existing job descriptions; and information on similar jobs provided by other employers.

The collection method and the resources available will affect determining who conducts the job analysis. More accurate data and greater acceptance of pay decisions usually result if the supervisor and the job incumbent are involved in the job analysis process.

Job Documentation

Most organizations with formalized pay programs use written job descriptions to document job content. Job descriptions may be defined as narrative statements of the nature and level of work being performed by persons occupying the job, as well as job specifications. Their exact content will be determined largely by the purpose or purposes for which they will be used. For example, information that is relevant to staffing, recruiting or test validation may not be required for compensation purposes, and vice versa.

Some computer-based job analysis methods result in job documentation that is not in narrative format, but the purpose and uses are the same. (Throughout this publication the term "job documentation" is used to include narrative, written descriptions and other systematic methods of documenting job content.)

Job documentation has five major uses in the design and administration of wage and salary programs:

- Job documentation is useful in *evaluating job content* and should be prepared with the evaluation criteria in mind. Before the relative value of jobs in an organization can be determined, the nature, purpose and organizational level of the jobs must be clearly understood. Principal duties and responsibilities, skill levels, and mental and physical effort required, as well as the conditions in which the work is performed, likewise must be clearly understood. A common shortcoming of job evaluation systems is the lack of quality information about the jobs.

- Job documentation also provides accurate data for making *pay comparisons* with other organizations. In gathering and analyzing salary survey data, a determination must be made as to whether jobs described in the survey are comparable to jobs in the organization. If so, it is valid to use the survey data. If no documentation exists, or if it is inaccurate, incomplete or outdated, then invalid comparisons and decisions may result.

- Job documentation also is used to provide *classification* control. In sound pay programs, employees are assigned to classifications (job titles) that are descriptive of their job duties. Thus employees are classified on the basis of actual work performed, rather than personal background or characteristics.

- Job documentation with clear definitions of job content provides effective *communication vehicles*, so employees and supervisors know what is to be accomplished. Once clear and accurate job documentation exists, it is much easier for employees and supervisors to set performance goals or standards and, subsequently, to review the employee's performance in light of these performance targets.

- Job documentation may be required when *third parties* request an explanation of the organization's decisions. Recent court cases show that government agencies charged with enforcing employee relations, labor relations and civil rights statutes frequently rely on job content analysis to determine the legality of human resources programs and practices. The existence of accurate, current, job-content-based documentation greatly will enhance an organization's ability to defend unwarranted charges of discrimination.

There are numerous other uses for job documentation outside of base pay plan administration, such as employee selection and orientation, training and development, and succession and career-path planning.

Job Documentation Components

There are a variety of formats for job documentation. Whatever the format, documentation should include the *nature* of the work (principle duties), the *level* of skill and responsibility required to perform the work, the types and amounts of mental and physical effort required, and the general physical environment in which the work is performed.

Written job descriptions typically will include at least the following sections:
- A job *identification* section including job title, department or location, date of completion and approvals
- A *general summary* or statement of job purpose
- A list of *principal* duties and *responsibilities* of the job.
- The *minimum* levels of knowledge, skills and abilities required to perform the work.

Rather than listing every conceivable task, major responsibility areas normally are highlighted (5 percent or more of time spent), with some indication of priority of duties or percent of time spent on each. In most cases, this means placing the highest/most important duty first, then those with decreased importance.

Some employers also choose to include some or all of the following information, either in the job description or in some other form of job documentation:
- Relevant *scope data*, such as budget, sales or profit responsibility, number of people supervised, etc.
- The nature and extent of *supervision* received and given
- The physical and mental *effort* required
- The *physical environment* in which the work is performed
- A disclaimer clause, stating that the job description does not necessarily include every task that an incumbent might perform.

Other Job Description Considerations

In narrative job descriptions, emphasis should be on brevity and clarity. Present tense and action verbs are normally used to enhance clarity. Potentially biased terminology should be avoided. If job specifications are included, they should be precise and verifiable, based on job content, not on the personal characteristics of the incumbent. Qualifications should reflect reasonable levels of knowledge, skills and abilities necessary for satisfactory job performance, not set at unrealistically high levels. Finally, job descriptions should be kept current to accurately reflect the jobs and to assist in any auditing process (internal or external).

Who should write the job description? To a great extent this depends upon the resources available to the organization. Whether prepared by the incumbent, the supervisor, a human resources specialist or a third party, the important thing is that the descriptions be well written. Line management may or may not participate in writing job descriptions, but it is important that it reviews and approves them.

Developing the Job Worth Hierarchy

In the early 1880s, Frederick W. Taylor assisted a steel company that was seeking a method to improve productivity. He designed a formal, systematic way of assigning pay to jobs, and his study became known as "job evaluation."

The 1923 Federal Classification Act was an initial attempt by Congress to establish a system for compensating federal white-collar employees fairly and systematically. It served to encourage the birth of a formal compensation-management approach that utilizes systematic methods for analyzing relative job value and compensation patterns within private and public organizations.

Merrill R. Lott designed the first point-factor job evaluation plan in the 1920s. This was followed in the late 1930s and early 1940s by the first factor-comparison method of evaluation, designed by Edward N. Hay, Eugene I. Benge and Samuel L.H. Burke. Since that time, numerous adaptations of the basic internal-evaluation techniques — slotting, ranking, classification, factor comparison, point factor — have been developed by academicians, management consultants and business organizations.

Over the years, the term "job evaluation" has taken on two meanings:

- To some compensation professionals, "job evaluation" is the *overall* process of comparing jobs in order to develop the job worth hierarchy. In this sense it contains the elements of both market pricing and internal job-content analysis, because internal and external comparisons are included.
- Many other compensation professionals, however, use the term in the more restricted sense of job *content evaluation*, developing a hierarchy based only on internal comparisons of job value.

Two basic methodologies historically have been used in developing a job worth hierarchy: one starting with and emphasizing market data; the other starting with and emphasizing job content. Each employer must determine which approach best suits the needs of its organization. To a great extent, the organization's pay philosophy; the number of distinct jobs; the sophistication of management; and the money available for design, installation and maintenance of the system will determine this. Each approach will be considered in turn.

Market Pricing

Although practically all systems recognize the role of the market in ranking jobs, some existing formal systems use market rates as the primary basis for establishing job worth. Benchmark jobs are chosen, priced from survey data and assigned relative values based on market pay levels. Benchmark jobs closely resemble other jobs performed in other organizations and/or across industries. Benchmark jobs should do the following:

- Be well-represented positions in the marketplace
- Be important in the organization's internal hierarchy
- Represent many organizational levels or grades in the salary structure(s) utilized by the company
- Be matched to 70 percent or more of the duties found in the survey jobs

- Generally have multiple incumbents, with the exception of managerial and executive-level positions within an organization.

All other jobs then are positioned in relation to these benchmarks. This process of positioning non-benchmark jobs is called slotting because it involves comparing or evaluating the value of the job not based on market factors (or points), but on its relative worth compared to other jobs that were priced in the market.

Benchmark jobs likewise can serve as internal anchor points for non-benchmark jobs. For example, a human resources assistant and an administrative assistant may be assigned to the same pay grade and salary range. These two benchmark jobs thus can be used to determine the relative value of other jobs assigned to that pay grade, for which market pay data are not available.

Job Content Evaluation Methods

Whichever basic approach is followed, most employers eventually face the task of determining the relative worth of one or more jobs on the basis of job content alone. This occurs early when the job content method is used — usually immediately after the job documentation has been prepared. With the market pricing approach, it occurs when no labor-market data is available to determine the positioning of non-benchmark jobs, and/or when management reconciles labor-market and job content data.

There is an almost limitless variety of evaluation methods emphasizing job content, but virtually all of them are modifications or derivatives of four basic methods. These four methods can be separated into two groups: quantitative and nonquantitative.

Nonquantitative — 'Whole Job' Evaluation

The two nonquantitative methods — *ranking* and *classification* — derive their nonquantitative label from the fact that they do not produce a precise numerical score for each job being evaluated. They do, however, assign each job a relative position in a job worth hierarchy. In measurement terms, they produce ordinal-level data only. Also called "whole-job" evaluation, these two nonquantitative methods determine relative worth of jobs on the basis of an overall or global assessment of job content. This is contrasted with the quantitative methods, wherein the evaluation of job content is based on a factor-by-factor evaluation of various aspects of job content.

- *Ranking* is perhaps the oldest, fastest and simplest of the classic methods of job evaluation. Evaluators rank jobs in order of their overall worth or value to the organization. The job the evaluators believe to be most valuable is placed first; the one they perceive as being worth least is ranked last, and so on. In this way a hierarchy is produced. There are many variations of this method. Some include instructing the evaluators to consider certain attributes of the jobs in their rankings. Another variation, *paired comparison*, compares each position to every other position (one at a time) and develops a "score" from the number of times a position is deemed more important than another position. The "score" is used to produce a ranking.

- The federal government originally developed *classification* during establishment of its pay program. A number of grades or levels are specified beforehand, and broad descriptions are written to delineate the characteristics of jobs to be placed in each of the grades. Each job then is evaluated by comparing the job documentation to the grade description, and the job is assigned to the grade that most closely describes the job characteristics.

Quantitative — 'Factor' Evaluation

The two broad categories of quantitative evaluation methods are the point-factor plans and job component. Each method evaluates job content on a factor-by-factor basis and produces a numerical score for each job evaluated.

- In the *point-factor* method, a number of factors are selected, such as those mentioned in factor comparison. These factors are weighted, and a scale of point values is assigned to each to reflect this weighting. Each job is compared to descriptions of the various levels or degrees within each factor. When the appropriate degree is selected for each factor, the assigned points are combined to produce a total score for each job.

- *Job component* is a quantitative job-content evaluation method that uses multiple regression and market data to establish the job worth hierarchy. Compensable factor data are collected on highly structured questionnaires for each job. These data are entered into a computer for benchmark jobs and then regressed against market data for those jobs. The resulting formula produced by the regression analysis is used to calculate the predicted value for both benchmark and non-benchmark jobs. Jobs are then arrayed in a hierarchy based on their predicted value.

Factor Selection and Weighting

All quantitative methods of job evaluation have one thing in common — a set of job factors that form the basis for evaluation. The choice and weighting of these factors is critical to the resulting job worth hierarchy. The selected factors should do the following:

- Represent all major aspects of job content for which the employer is willing to pay (compensable factors) — typically skill, effort, responsibility and working conditions (or subfactors of these broad universal factors)
- Avoid excessive overlap
- Be definable and measurable
- Be easily understood by employees and administrators
- Be relatively simple to evaluate, without requiring excessive installation or administrative cost

- Be selected with legal considerations in mind.

It is difficult to choose one set of compensable factors that can be applied to the entire organization, top to bottom, or to jobs with far different job content, such as production jobs, clerical jobs and management jobs. However, if more than one set of factors or systems is used, care should be taken to ensure that no job, or group of jobs, will have its position in the job worth hierarchy distorted by the set of factors or systems used in the evaluation process.

The weights assigned to the factors should be determined by the employer's judgment of their relative importance to the organization. Factor definitions and degrees should be written in a clear, easily understood manner. These definitions should be as specific as possible, and the degrees available should represent all of those needed to logically evaluate the jobs that will be included in the system.

The compensable factors included in most existing job evaluation plans are really "subfactors" of skill, effort, responsibility and working conditions. Care should be taken to avoid subfactors that are duplicative or so greatly overlapping that they cause an overweighting of one of the principal factors.

Who Should Perform the Evaluation

The job evaluation process can be performed in a number of different ways, depending to a great extent on the size and nature of the organization. Senior management may evaluate jobs in a smaller organization, while committees of lower-level managers typically assist in this process as the organization grows. Staff specialists are often used in larger organizations.

Other Considerations

Experience suggests that a successful job evaluation process can be facilitated by the following:

- Including incumbents (of the types of jobs being evaluated) in some part of the evaluation process
- Establishing an appeal procedure whereby supervisors or employees who disagree with job grade assignments may voice their concerns
- Communicating the basic elements of the evaluation system to the employees, including an explanation that the system is based on internal and external considerations, to establish credibility of the system with employees
- Installing procedures for a periodic (usually annual) internal audit. The procedures need not be complicated or time-consuming and could well begin by assessing employee complaints about the system. An analysis of turnover statistics and exit interviews can also be very helpful in isolating potential problem areas. Several questions should be asked about the application of the job evaluation system:

- Is training provided to those involved in the job evaluation process?
- Are written instruction or guidelines provided?
- Are job evaluation decisions made or reviewed by more than one person?
- Is there inter-rater reliability?
- Are persons in protected classes involved in the decision-making process?
- Are the decision makers representative of organizational entities and a cross-section of employees?
- Have the factors been applied consistently to all of the evaluated jobs?
- Have changes in the organization or the workforce lessened the appropriateness of the methods and procedures used?

Finally, several additional points should be considered regarding the design of *quantitative* evaluation plans:

- Is there a defensible rationale for the choice and weighting of factors?
- Has the weighting of the factors been statistically analyzed to preclude the use of factors that overlap or are irrelevant?
- Have degree-level definitions been consistently and logically defined for each factor?
- Are there unused or little-used degrees within any factor that are superfluous?
- Do the factors fairly represent the content of jobs held by both men and women?
- Are the factors limited to skills, physical and mental effort, responsibility and working conditions or subfactors thereof? If not, are they defensible?

Pay-Data Collection and Analysis
Pay-Data Collection

There are a number of valid and reliable methods of market pay-data collection and analysis in common use; some are formal, others informal.

Before collecting pay data, an organization should define its relevant labor market, which typically varies by job group and may consist of the following:

- Similar organizations in the local labor market
- All employers in the local market
- Similar organizations in the regional or national market
- All employers in the regional or national market.

(See Figure 3-2 on page 42.)

Employers will want to use surveys that include data from other employers with whom the organization competes in the labor market. Therefore, this survey sample may vary between different groups of jobs. Typically, considerations include the geographic area, size of the organization, employee relations practices, profitability

(if relevant), industry type, organizational structure and other factors deemed pertinent to the job group to be surveyed. Because this selection process requires a great deal of care so that an appropriate labor market is sampled, it is usually helpful to determine the sources of new employees and where employees go when they voluntarily leave the organization.

The organization next decides whether it will conduct the salary survey, use a consulting firm, subscribe to or purchase commercially available surveys, use data available through services such as the Bureau of Labor Statistics, local chambers of commerce, employer associations or online (Internet) applications. Organizations base these decisions on the cost of securing the data, time constraints, reliability of the data, the need to control the quality of the data collected and the necessity of keeping the data confidential. The survey can be conducted by the following methods:

- Telephone interviews
- A mailed questionnaire
- A personal visit to the company to be surveyed
- A meeting of all participating organizations to discuss the job matches
- Any combination of the above.

Conducting the survey itself will give the organization more control over data collection and analysis, but it also may be the most expensive and time-consuming choice. Additionally, when conducting the survey the organization needs to be cognizant of the Sherman Anti-Trust Act and any potential implications. When the organization conducts its survey, it may limit the number of participants willing to provide data. Also, when surveys are used in collective bargaining, the individual employer may be required to reveal data that is considered confidential by survey participants. It is for these reasons that many organizations decide to use third-party sources.

Another decision to be made by the surveying organization is the type of pay data to be collected. Depending on the degree of sophistication desired, the surveying organization will determine whether it is concerned with total rewards or some combination of the elements of total rewards — base pay, other cash, benefits, perquisites or work-life issues. Some surveys may request an array of individual pay rates for benchmark jobs while others will request only summary data, such as the means (averages) or medians (middle values) of pay for benchmark jobs within each participating organization. Many surveys will also ask for the established pay grade range for benchmark jobs. Some surveys gather additional data such as job tenure, education attainment, number of people supervised, etc.

Finally, the employer will select the benchmark jobs for which data are to be collected. Job descriptions and survey questionnaires will be prepared and potential survey participants will be contacted.

Based upon this brief description of the process of collecting pay data, it should be apparent that the process is, and should be, neutral with respect to the sex or race of employees included in the data.

Analysis of the Collected Market Data

Once pay data is gathered, the organization must determine the depth of analysis required to meet its needs. While some organizations might simply determine the average market pay rate and approximate it within its own salary structure, others may choose to utilize more sophisticated analytical techniques. At a minimum, this process requires the computation of the going market rate (average or median) for the organization's benchmark jobs.

Formal analytical techniques involve the science of statistical sampling: the study of relationships existing among selected items that form a specific group (the sample) and are representative of the entire group (the population). The objective is to provide a data sample that accurately describes the larger universe.

Another decision is whether or not the data should be weighted; and if so, how? Some data may be more relevant (or representative of the organization's jobs) than other data. Pay rates for each employer can be averaged; or they may be weighted by the number of incumbents. One employer may have a disproportionate number of the jobs or employees, and pay far above or far below the going rate for all other organizations. A weighting may be applied to that employer's data so that a more representative sample is obtained. In most surveys this is referred to as the weighted mean (or median). If an organization is utilizing more than one survey, it may believe one survey is a better representation of the job within the organization, and may choose to weigh that survey more heavily. Additionally, with today's hybrid jobs, organizations are finding that more than one job listed in a survey reflects a hybrid job within the organization. Based upon this "blended" job in the organization, the data will need to be blended (or weighted appropriately).

The measures most commonly used to depict a "typical going rate" are means and medians. The range of values, which is often divided into quartiles, is also quite useful. Many compensation practitioners believe the interquartiles (the middle 50 percent, between the 25th and 75th percentile) are the most useful, because they exclude any wide swings of data at either the upper or lower extremes; others may select a broader range (for example, the 10th to 90th percentile). Eliminating a portion of the data to eliminate extremes is referred to as trimming the data. When computing the average for trimmed data, the result is known as a trimmed mean.

Base Pay Structure 4

Setting Rates and/or Ranges for Jobs

A pay structure is established by setting the rates of pay for the jobs in the job worth hierarchy. In setting these rates, a number of major policy issues should be considered. First off, how should the organization's pay levels relate to the market?

In most organizations, a compensation philosophy defines the competitive market position an organization will take with its compensation programs. The three most common competitive market positions are lead, lag and lead-lag.

The first option an organization has regarding competitive market position is to **lead** the market (See Figure 4-1). When an organization leads the market, it consciously sets its pay structure at year-end anticipated market level, not at the current market levels. The organization's pay levels will then "lead" the market until the start of the next year. In other words, the company will start the year ahead of its competition and remain there until the end of the year, when market rates catch up. When an organization uses this method of competitive market position, the organization is usually seen as a "pay leader." The organizations that typically lead the market will look for experienced talent and attract that talent by paying higher-than-market wages.

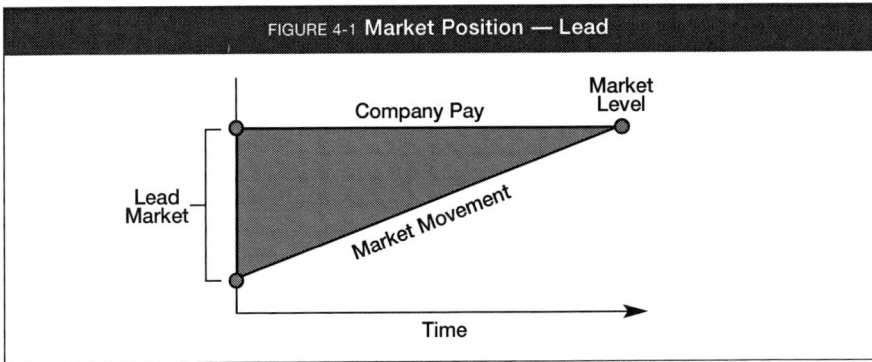

FIGURE 4-1 **Market Position — Lead**

The second option for an organization is to **lag** the market (See Figure 4-2 on page 48). When an organization lags the market, it consciously sets its pay structure equal to current market levels at the *beginning* of the year. With this scenario, the organization's pay levels will "lag" the market as the year progresses. Typically, an

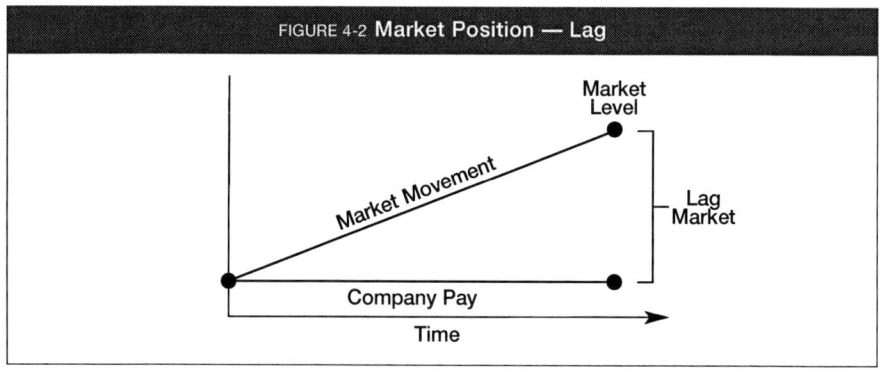

FIGURE 4-2 **Market Position — Lag**

organization that lags the market will choose to hire less experienced applicants and pay less than market wages. The organization may offer additional training and development opportunities as a means to attract and develop employees.

The third option an organization has is **Lead-Lag** (See Figure 4-3). When an organization is using a lead-lag philosophy, it consciously sets its pay structure at midyear anticipated market level. By doing this, the organization's pay levels will "lead" the market in the first half of the year and "lag" the market in the second half. Typically, an organization that uses a lead-lag philosophy will attempt to hire more qualified applicants than lag organizations, but offer more training and development opportunities than lead organizations.

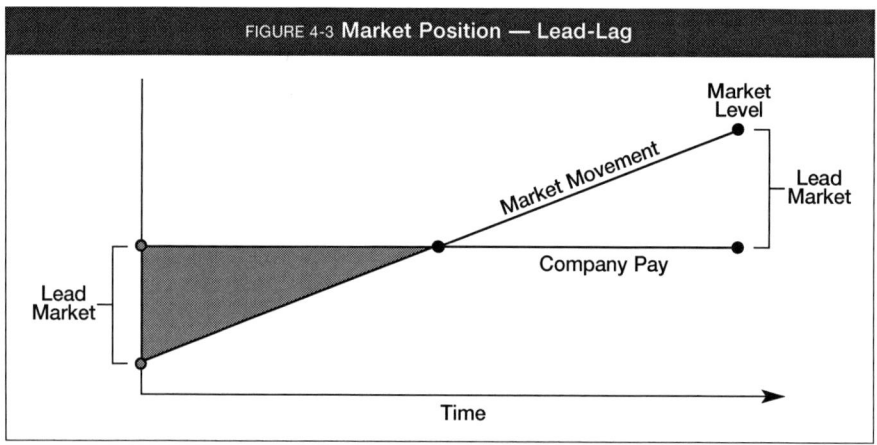

FIGURE 4-3 **Market Position — Lead-Lag**

After the compensation philosophy is determined, the compensation strategy will be developed. A compensation strategy includes the principles that guide the design, implementation and administration of a compensation program. Some strategies also specify which programs will be used and how those programs will be administered. A typical compensation strategy is intended to ensure the compensation programs will support the business strategy of the organization. The compensation strategy

will guide the organization on what it is willing to pay for. Some examples include the following:
- Job content
- Seniority
- Performance
- Skills
- Cost of living
- A combination of the above.

It will also guide the organization on how it pays its employees.
- A single-rate structure (all employees on a given job receive the same pay)
- A time-progression structure, or step increase (progression through a pay range based solely on time in the job)
- A range structure with progression based on merit
- A combination of time-progression and merit, with automatic progression to a certain point in the range, and further progression within the range based on merit
- A pay system based solely on productivity
- A pay system based on the acquisition of new skills
- A combination of the above
- A pay system that provides for long- or short-term incentives, in addition to base pay
- Steps the organization should take to ensure that pay is administered in a bias-free manner.

Having decided the major policy questions, the pay structure and pay-delivery system can then be created.

Pay Structure

If pay grades are utilized, the number of grades is typically influenced by one or both of the following factors:
- The number of different levels of relative job value that are recognized by the organization;
- The difference in pay between the highest- and lowest-paid jobs in the pay structure.

To determine whether the proper number of grades has been established, an employer should determine whether the jobs in each grade should have the same range, or jobs in different grades warrant different pay ranges.

After the pay grade has been determined for each job through the job evaluation process, an organization can proceed to develop its *pay ranges* around each of its job grades. (See Figure 4-4 on page 50.)

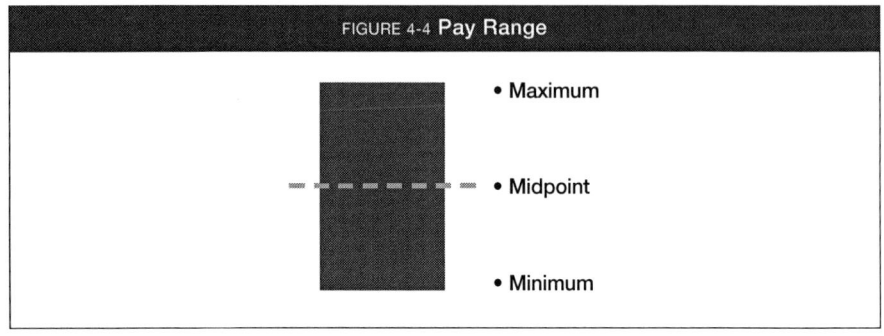

Pay-range *midpoints* usually are the focal points in the development of pay ranges, particularly in non-union systems. A midpoint most often is defined as the market "going rate" for jobs assigned to that grade. Midpoints actually will reflect the organizations' policies regarding the relationship of their pay trends to the market; for example, whether they lead, lag or lead-lag competitive pay rates. Because pay ranges are developed from historical pay data and are designed to last for some predetermined amount of time, it is not uncommon for the midpoint of a range to be the *prospective* market going rate. It is up to the organization to determine the desired lifetime of its pay structure and how much future market pay-rate growth it will build into its pay-structure midpoints. Many organizations utilize the midpoints of pay ranges to determine frequency of pay increase as well as size. For these reasons, the determination of pay-range midpoints can be a critical factor in maintaining a competitive pay position within the labor market.

An organization can determine its pay-range midpoints by simply averaging the market rates for benchmark jobs in each grade. Or it may use more sophisticated techniques such as linear regression. The organization can plot a trend line of its own pay rates, compare it to the competitive pay trend line and determine what is necessary to achieve the desired competitive position within the labor market.

Having determined the midpoints of its pay ranges, an organization will then develop its pay range minimums and maximums. The pay range *minimum* is usually the lowest pay rate that an organization plans to pay for jobs in a particular pay grade. Employees hired at the pay-range minimum usually possess minimal qualifications for their jobs. The pay-range minimums should also be competitive with what other organizations are willing to pay to hire employees to fill jobs at that level. Pay rates below the pay-range minimum are referred to as *green circle rates*. Green circle rates may result from the following:

- Poor performance
- Range increases
- Company policy of starting trainees at a probationary rate below the minimum.

Green circle rates normally are temporary anomalies that are resolved either by attrition or by an eventual increase in the employee's pay rate to the pay-range minimum.

A pay-range *maximum* is typically defined as the highest rate an employer is willing to pay for jobs in that grade. The range maximum recognizes, in a structural way, that there is a limit of worth for any job, above which the organization will not ordinarily pay.

Organizations will usually strive to keep all pay rates within the established pay ranges, but in some cases they may decide to pay either above the pay-range maximum or below the minimum. Rates paid above the maximum are referred to as *red circle rates*. Red circle rates may occur as a result of the following:

- An employee's demotion from a job in a higher pay range (with no reduction in pay)
- Changes in job content causing the job to be re-evaluated at a lower level
- A pay increase granted to an exceptional employee who has reached a career plateau or whose skills are in very short supply
- The result of the organization not following its own pay-administration policies (for example, ignoring the range maximums).

(See Figure 4-5, below.)

In determining grades and salary ranges, the organization must consider things such as the following:

- Range spread (the percentage difference between the minimum and maximum of a given pay range)
- The amount of range overlap, if any, desired between adjacent pay ranges.

There are many schools of thought on how to approach these two issues. Organizations should form their own policies, taking into consideration issues such as the following:

- Promotional practices
- Union status
- Salary compression

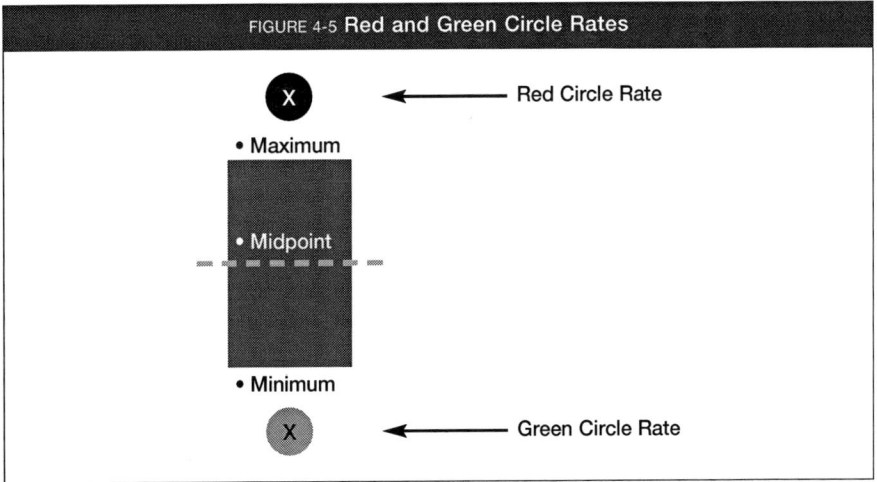

FIGURE 4-5 **Red and Green Circle Rates**

- Key pay grades resulting from labor shortages or high turnover
- Pay grades that constitute career plateaus.

The resulting pay structure should reflect the following:
- The organizational objectives
- The organization's philosophy on how it will relate pay to the market
- Internal relative job values
- Total rewards mix
- Compensation policies, practices and procedures
- The employer's approach to organizational structure
- The economic ability of the organization to pay at a given level.

Once the pay-range structure has been developed, the organization must decide how it will move employees through the pay range. Many organizations use individual performance as the basis for movement through the pay range. Others use an automatic (or step) progression approach based upon employee tenure. Still others provide cost-of-living increases tied to various inflation indices. Many organizations use a combination of these and other methods.

After an employer has established one or more pay structures (hierarchies of pay grades and ranges), a number of other policy issues must be addressed. Some of the most important of these are as follows:

- What should the starting rates be for new hires?
- How should employees move from the minimums to the maximums of the pay ranges established for their jobs?
- How should a pay increase be determined for an employee who is being promoted from one job to another?
- What influence, if any, should increases in going market rates, and increases in the cost of living, have on the determination of pay increases for individuals?

Each organization must develop its own answers to these questions and establish policies and procedures to facilitate consistent practices throughout the organization.

Broadbanding

Broadbanding has been a part of the HR field since the late '80s and early '90s and was developed to compress many salary grades into fewer, wide pay "bands." Those organizations that implemented such a system were driven by the need to adapt salary administration systems and procedures to meet a new business climate and create a flatter organization.

Broadbanding can be defined as a pay structure that consolidates a large number of pay grades and salary ranges into much fewer broadbands with relatively wide salary ranges, typically with 100-percent (or more) differences between minimum and maximum. Simply stated, broadbanding refers to the collapsing of job clusters or tiers of positions into a few wide bands to manage career growth and deliver pay.

Broadbanding was created to help achieve several objectives, namely the following:
- Develop broader workforce skills.
- Encourage career development among employees.
- Reduce administration of job evaluation, salary structure and merit pay.

Broadbanding usually appeals to fast-moving organizations that are undergoing persistent change. Such organizations that want to be quicker and more flexible in the marketplace have implemented broadbanding. They have found that broadbands complement processes designed to increase company speed, flexibility and risk taking.

Some or most of the career-ladder rungs were removed and employees were encouraged to earn more by adding value to the company. This could be accomplished by developing new skills or competencies and/or participating in a variable pay system with a line of sight to the company's performance.

Broadbands support this evolving organizational dynamic by providing less formal structure. The traditional compensation approach emphasized internal equity and focused employees' attention on the world inside the firm, and broadbanding helps them experience an internal culture that more closely reflects the external,

---

SIDEBAR: **Broadbanding Is Not for Everyone**

This is not to say that broadbanding is a panacea for all organizations. One potential disadvantage is that broadbanding's delayered approach to salary administration may not fit the culture of heavily level-oriented companies. The need to manage salaries also does not go away. Market pricing becomes even more important because it is used extensively to identify salary targets.

When broadbanding is implemented, an organization may also have to re-examine things such as management incentives, perquisites and other items tied to the conventional salary grade. Line managers also may need to be retrained to make compensation decisions while being persuaded to accept new or greater responsibility for employee career development.

As some companies have found, pay systems are most effective when they support organizational change, not when they lead change. Some theorize if an organization is not ready for broadbanding, it will likely fail.

Other potential pitfalls exist:
- It could be possible to flatten the pay structure to the extent that supervisors and their subordinates are in the same band.
- The question of inflation arises, both of pay and of expectations, when employees are put in bands with potentially higher maximums than their previous grade maximums.
- It becomes more difficult to compare jobs to the marketplace and maintain external equity.

competitive marketplace. It helps make it easier for them to reorient themselves to the marketplace.

In broadbanding, there is no automatic progression to the midpoint because there is no midpoint. The marketplace for talent is no longer represented by highly defined salary structures, but rather mirrored by loosely defined, ambiguous broadbands that do not directly apply to an employee's position.

Starting Rates of Pay

When pay ranges have been formally established, it is the policy of most employers to pay new hires who appear to have only the minimum qualifications for their jobs, at or near the range minimum. The objective is to avoid paying them at rates that are too close to those paid to more experienced employees in the same job. Occasionally, supply and demand conditions are such that new hires with relatively little experience must be paid substantially above the range minimums. Additionally, individuals with substantial experience (or otherwise superior qualifications) frequently are hired at higher levels in the rate ranges.

Increases to Base Rates of Pay

Today's employees typically are eligible for several types of base pay increases, such as general (or across-the-board) increases, cost-of-living increases, promotion increases and within-range increases, such as step increases and merit increases.

General (or across-the-board) increases are those that are granted in equal percentages or equal dollar amounts to all employees in an eligible group. For example, all employees might receive pay increases equal to 25 cents per hour, or 3 percent of their current pay. Employers might specify that some employees (for example, those who exceed the maximums of their rate ranges or those whose performance is unacceptable) are to be excluded from receiving such increases. General increases are not conceptually compatible with pay-for-performance programs, and the use of general increases has diminished as performance-based programs have expanded.

A *cost-of-living increase* is a specific type of general increase that is typically awarded in equal cents per hour or percentage terms to all employees in a pay program or structure. Cost-of-living allowance (COLA) increases, however, are intended to protect employees' purchasing power against erosion caused by inflation. These increases typically relate to increases in the Consumer Price Index (CPI). Thus, all cost-of-living increases are general increases, but not all general increases are cost-of-living increases.

Promotion increases are increases granted to employees who are promoted from one job to another job with a higher pay grade and range. The size of increase is usually influenced by the magnitude of the promotion (as measured by the difference between the pay ranges assigned to the promotee's old and new jobs) and the pay relationships among the promotee's peers, superiors and subordinates.

Within-range increases are types of base pay increases that move employees forward in the pay ranges assigned to their jobs. Within-range pay increases are virtually always determined by some combination of the employees' length of service and performance. The two principal types of within-range increases are as follows:

1. *Increases based primarily on length of service* (though differences in performance may also be reflected). These may be step increases, whereby the pay ranges are divided into a number of pay rates with increases related to length of service. The step-increase concept is used most commonly for nonexempt employees, and there are several different approaches to this concept:

   a. The first is for *length of service only*. Here the employee receives single step increases up to the range maximum, which is usually at or just above the competitive market rate. If performance is unsatisfactory, the increase is denied and probation, demotion or dismissal may result.

   b. The second reflects both *length of service* and *performance*. One approach is illustrated in the following table:

Performance Rating	Pay Action
Outstanding	2-step increase
Exceeds standards	1-step increase; may accelerate timing of next review
Meets standards	1-step increase
Does not meet standards	No increase

   c. Another approach involves *two or three performance tracks* through which the employee progresses to a performance zone maximum. The number of steps can be increased to allow for smaller percentage steps.

   d. Finally, it is possible to add *timing* differences. This further accentuates differences in pay level based upon differences in performance.

2. *Increases based on merit* usually are administered in the form of a range of percentages for varying levels of performance. As mentioned earlier, they also may be used in combination with step-progression increases.

   Inherent in most merit-increase programs are the following notions:

   - The speed with which employees move through pay ranges will be determined principally, if not solely, on the basis of their job performance.
   - Performance will also determine how far employees are allowed to progress in their pay ranges.

Thus in determining merit increases, many organizations consider the performance of the individual and his or her current rate in the pay range. As a result, the merit increase may vary in size and timing.

Many organizations use a fixed frequency and vary the increase's size. The fixed frequency may vary by job level, but the most typical frequency at all levels is 12 months.

Timing of increases is sometimes based on the pay policy year (focal point) or the anniversary (anniversary date) of the employee's service or last increase date.

A smaller but significant percentage of organizations varies the size of the increase and the frequency. A minority of organizations fixes the size of the increase, but varies the frequency.

The size of the increase (typically measured as a percent increase) generally varies directly with the individual's performance (the better the performance the bigger the increase) and, inversely, with the employee's position in the pay range (the lower the position in the range, the bigger the increase as a percent of current pay). It is common practice to provide supervisors and managers with increase-planning guidelines. These guideline charts include a range of options to allow managerial flexibility.

A final variation on the above methods involves either step-progression or percent-merit guideline increases to the range midpoint, with a lump-sum bonus given that varies in amount, depending upon performance.

There are, of course, many variations of these pay-increase approaches. Basically, however, all known variations of in-range pay increases are some combination of these two basic approaches — step increases or merit increases.

Merit Pay Considerations

Compensation professionals believe certain conditions generally must exist for performance-based pay-increase programs to be successful:

- Individual differences in job performance should be measurable.
- Individual differences in job performance must be significant enough to warrant the time and effort required to measure them and relate pay to them.
- The pay range should be sufficiently broad (35 percent to 50 percent) to allow for adequate differentiation of pay based upon performance, and/or level of experience and skill.
- Supervisors and managers must be trained in employee-performance planning and appraisal.
- Management must be committed, and employees must be receptive, to making distinctions in pay based upon performance.
- Managers must be adequately skilled in managing pay.
- Sufficient control systems must be implemented to ensure that merit increase guidelines are followed.

There are potential productivity and incentive benefits to be derived from the implementation of a performance-based pay-increase program. However, this type of program is more complex to administer and requires more difficult management decisions. Compensation professionals must ensure that their merit pay programs measure performance as objectively as possible. Management must carefully evaluate performance and make judgments regarding pay differentials. Significant commitments of time and effort are required by all involved in this process.

Performance Appraisal Considerations

For a performance-based pay system to meet its objectives, a well-designed and properly administered performance-management system must exist. An effective performance-management system includes the following characteristics:

- Performance is appraised on the basis of direct measurement of each employee's output or results. For example, the quantity and quality of work is assessed rather than the employee personality traits. Employee behavior is considered only to the extent that it is job related and affects job results.
- Supervisors are trained in the concepts and the process involved in appraising performance.
- Measures or criteria used are as objective and quantitative as possible to minimize the potential for varying interpretations by different reviewers.
- Objective performance standards are established for various levels of employee performance when practical.
- The relative importance (weight) of each of the performance criteria is established.
- When practical, employees are involved in the determination of performance criteria, standards and weights to ensure greater acceptance of the program.
- Performance criteria, standards and weights are communicated to the employee at the beginning of the appraisal period, and periodically reviewed and updated for timeliness, relevance and utility.
- The appraisal is written, and discussed by the employee and supervisor. The employee is involved in the process prior to finalizing the written appraisal. (Many organizations make a copy of the written appraisal available to the employee and provide an appeals mechanism for reconciling differences between employee and supervisor.)
- Finally, the appraisal process is audited routinely and frequently, to identify and eliminate potential problems.

Communication of the Pay Program 5

Many aspects of human resources are not well understood by employees, from how pay is determined to why a company conducts salary surveys or provides certain benefits plans. Maintaining the proper balance between the administrative demands of the program, the communications needs of employees and the fiscal responsibilities to the organization have long been a challenge to HR professionals.

For employees, pay delivers a strong message. Many studies have shown pay consistently ranks as a top reason for staying with an organization. Compensation can be a powerful motivator or an equally powerful de-motivator, depending upon how it is used. Getting everyone on the same page will eliminate confusion caused by secrecy, infrequent communications and crossed signals.

A major component to communicating pay actions is to clarify the expectations and increase employee awareness of what is required. Employees expect communication pertaining to the pay program will be as follows:

- Honest
- Thorough
- Understandable
- Relevant.

While communicating pay actions to employees, one must always remember to describe it simply and briefly from the employee perspective. Additionally, the communicator must remember to focus on the main elements of the pay action. These main elements will include the following:

- The reason behind the pay action
- How the pay action will be processed
- When the pay action will become effective
- Whether the pay action will be permanent (or just a temporary action)
- Whether the pay action will be in a lump-sum or a periodic action.

When communicating pay actions, one must be cognizant of the communicator. It would not be recommended to have a fellow department member notify employees of a market increase. One needs to examine the information being communicated and chose the appropriate communicator. The appropriate communicator could be one of the following:

- HR manager
- Director
- Department manager
- Supervisor.

The appropriate communicator should be chosen based upon the specific pay action and the audience. For the pay system to influence work behaviors and attitudes, the workforce must understand it. To relate pay messages to employees in a lasting manner, the supervisor is usually the most effective channel to use and should be the center of the communications effort. Employees' perceptions about the organization's pay system are shaped through dialogue with their managers and via formal and informal communications programs. Ongoing communication with employees enhances the effectiveness and acceptance of the pay program and helps reduce misperceptions. Conducting "train the trainer" sessions will help supervisors communicate pay information to employees.

For any program to succeed, it must be relentlessly communicated to the workforce. In today's competitive business environment, many companies have abandoned secrecy about their pay program in favor of conveying information to their employees. Information about pay ranges and merit budgets is increasingly made public by organizations. A major part of every compensation professional's job nowadays is answering questions about the compensation program and trying to get management and employee buy-in. When communicating pay information on employees, you need to tell them and *sell* them on the program.

Staying on Top of Program Administration

The job's not done until the paperwork is finished. However, with the case of pay programs, that is never the case. Paperwork is a component of the ongoing part of pay maintenance.

To keep the pay program running like a well-oiled machine, in light of continual changes within the organization and in the labor market, compensation professionals should follow these guidelines:

- Objectives are clearly stated; policies and procedures should be established and communicated
- Proper controls are in place to ensure that policies and procedures are consistently applied
- There is adequate support for the compensation function, including sufficient staff and other resources, as well as top management buy-in to ensure the pay program is administered fairly

- The compensation staff properly performs administrative activities
- The pay program is audited regularly to ensure effectiveness and compliance.

Checklist: Subjects Frequently Included
- Objectives of the pay program
- The targeted competitive position of the organization's pay levels
- Methods used to define and determine the value of jobs
- The role of individual performance in the pay program (how performance is measured, how frequently and by whom)
- How pay-increase amounts are determined
- The effect of economic constraints and government regulations on distribution of available funds to employees
- Polices, procedures and controls used to administer the pay program on an ongoing basis.

Techniques that facilitate communication include the following:
- Written policy statements
- Oral presentations to employee groups
- Direct discussion between supervisors and employees
- Supervisory training in performance appraisal and pay administration
- Distribution of procedure manuals that describe how the pay program operates
- Individualized status reports to employees
- Ongoing written communications on current topics via employee newsletters, intranets or other in-house publications.

The methods used for communication will depend to a great extent on the management style of the organization, the general employee relations atmosphere, and the resources management is able and willing to commit.

Maintaining and Auditing the Pay Program 6

Maintenance of pay programs is one of the most critical elements of sound base pay administration. Unless programs are properly maintained, errors occur and inequities will eventually undermine program effectiveness. The maintenance of pay programs is inherently difficult, due to the following:

- Continual changes in the content of the various jobs in an organization
- Continual changes in the going market rates for jobs
- Frequent changes in organizational structure and staffing levels
- The ever-evolving and expanding regulatory framework governing pay programs
- The inevitable turnover within the compensation function itself.

Keys to Successful Pay-Program Maintenance

There are five keys to the proper maintenance of pay programs:

- Clearly stated objectives, policies and procedures are established and communicated.
- Proper controls are operative to ensure policies and procedures are being consistently applied.
- There is adequate support for the compensation function itself — including provision of sufficient staff and other resources, as well as the top management support necessary to ensure that the pay program is administered with fairness and integrity.
- The compensation staff properly performs administrative activities.
- The pay program is routinely audited for effectiveness and efficiency.

This chapter focuses on the ongoing administrative activities necessary for maintaining pay programs and the types of audits that can be conducted to ensure that the programs are functioning properly.

Ongoing Administrative Activities

The proper maintenance of base pay programs requires continual analysis of the content and requirements for the various jobs in an organization. The information collected in the course of these ongoing analyses requires careful documentation by job descriptions, completed position analysis questionnaires or some combination thereof.

Changes in organizational structure and staffing levels also affect the content of jobs and their relative worth to the organization. Unless job documentation is properly maintained and jobs are properly evaluated, employees may be assigned incorrect job titles, pay grades and or pay ranges. To ensure ongoing program success, some organizations undertake regular reviews or "desk audits" of various organizational components. Others attempt to verify job content information throughout the process of performance planning and appraisal.

Compensation professionals also continually monitor the position of the organization's pay levels vis-à-vis those of the competition. Thus, compensation professionals participate in, purchase and extract data from pay surveys. This compiled data, as well as the organization's pay philosophy and ability to pay, combine to produce decisions regarding changes in pay structures and budgets. If the monitoring of the market is neglected or poorly performed, an organization's pay rates and/or rate ranges may be too high (causing excessive financial costs) or too low (causing excessive employee relations costs) when compared with those of competitors.

In addition to pay-structure maintenance activities, compensation professionals create pay-increase budgets, planning documents, authorization procedures and guidelines that combine to support the organization's pay philosophy. They also prepare periodic reports for top management regarding pay-program results and costs.

Pay-Program Audits

Systematic pay-program audits can be invaluable for ensuring an organization's compensation program is being properly administered and maintained. Observers of human behavior have noted "people do what is inspected, not necessarily what is expected." In the absence of audits, polices may become wishes and pay programs may be rendered ineffective due to inconsistent practices and resultant inequities, charges of illegal discrimination, employee dissatisfaction or excessive costs.

The first step in preparing for and conducting pay-program audits is deciding what to audit. In general, pay-program audits include some combination of four different types of measures:

- *Process measures* are used to determine the extent to which the pay program is being smoothly and efficiently administered. Some sample measures would be as follows:
  - Productivity of staff
  - Satisfaction of line managers with the administration of the pay program
  - Cost of analytical/data-collection activities
  - Job analysis
  - Job documentation
  - Job evaluation

- Survey data
- Amount of management time required for pay-program administration
- Cost of data processing/consulting support
- Error rates in databases
- Backlog of requests for evaluations/re-evaluations
- Timeliness of pay-increase planning and processing
- Timeliness of quality of performance-appraisal data.

- *Policy compliance measures* are used to determine if the pay program is being administered in accordance with policy. Several examples would be as follows:
  - Actual rates and ranges versus market position specified by policy
  - Pay position in range
  - Percent of employees outside pay ranges
    - Green circle
    - Red circle.
  - Extent of compliance with salary-increase policies
  - Extent of compliance with starting-rate policies
  - Job title congruence with actual job content
  - Validity of job evaluation data
  - Consistency of pay grade and range assignments with job evaluation results
  - Compliance with performance-appraisal policies and procedures
  - Quality of performance-appraisal information.

- *Documentation adequacy measures* are used to determine the extent to which the program is committed to writing. Consider the following:
  - Percent of jobs for which accurate and up-to-date documentation exists
  - Percent of jobs with accurate job evaluation documentation
  - Percent of jobs with valid pay-grade assignments
  - Percent of employees' files containing current performance-appraisal documents
  - Compliance with Fair Labor Standards Act (FLSA)/Equal Pay Act (EPA) recordkeeping requirements
  - Existence of written policies regarding
    - The design and operation of the job evaluation procedures
    - The operation of performance-appraisal procedures
    - Pay increases
    - Structure-adjustment procedures
    - Re-evaluation procedures.

- *Overall results measures* are used to assess how well pay programs achieve the established goals, such as the following:
  - Attraction and retention of qualified employees
    - Number of openings
    - Duration of openings
    - Quality of employees
    - Number of terminations (voluntary and involuntary).
  - Compliance with applicable laws and regulations
    - Grievances
    - Lawsuits
    - Statistical analyses.
  - Results of performance-based pay polices
    - Turnover by performance level
    - Percent of payroll allocated in a performance-dependent manner
    - Correlation between pay and performance levels.
  - Protection of the organization's financial resources
    - Pay as a percent of operating budget
      - Historical
      - Product competitors.
  - Organization rates versus market rates.
  - Employee perceptions of
    - Internal equity
      - In the same job
      - In different jobs.
    - External equity.

The second step in preparing for and conducting pay-program audits is to *select the participants*. Participants should understand audit principles and processes, and possess well-developed analytical, writing and interpersonal skills. In addition, they should be disinterested parties that have no stake in a particular audit outcome.

The third step is to *develop a data collection and analysis plan*. Interviews or opinion surveys can be used to determine how various parties view the pay program. Auditors also can examine a wide variety of internal and external records and reports, including human resources records, payroll data, pay-survey data, accounting records and compensation databases.

The fourth step is to *assemble the necessary data* to support the analysis.

The fifth step is to *analyze the collected data* and *develop findings and recommendations*. The audit report should present findings in an objective manner and provide adequate information to give readers the proper perspective.

Management's role is to do as follows:

- Review audit results and recommendations.
- Prioritize the improvements that are required.
- Allocate the necessary resources.
- Follow up to ensure that the work is completed.

Organizations often find that audits are useful tools for educating management groups about the intricacies of pay-program administration, thus increasing their understanding of and support for the pay program.

Considering the size of base pay expenditures in many organizations, it is generally appropriate to conduct comprehensive audits at least every two years. This approach will ensure organizations are continually aware of the extent to which pay programs achieve their objectives so problems can be identified and resolved as quickly as possible.

Current Trends 7

As the compensation function continues to evolve several new trends are beginning to show. The first six chapters of this book focus on the foundations of base pay programs, whereas this chapter will discuss compensation trends.

Hot Skills

Amid rapid changes in the labor market, organizations need to keep a close eye on how their competitors are paying their employees and how they are handling hot skills positions. Hot skills employees, such as knowledge workers and those with certain IT skills (and those in the health care industry, namely nurses) are in high demand. As pay continues to escalate, organizations struggle with attracting and retaining these hot-skills positions.

As the demand continues to increase, some organizations are redesigning the total rewards mix to both attract and retain these employees. Hot skills are critical to organizations and, as long as they are in short supply and demand is high, they will continue to drive up pay for those skill sets. As organizations mature in their understanding of the total rewards model and how that model can flex to attract and retain employees, more and more organizations will begin to utilize a modified model for hot skills.

Part of the total rewards package modification could be to increase the frequency of pay increases. Some organizations might offer more frequent increases to hot-skills employees in order to retain them. These additional increases are usually smaller in amount (versus the annual increases of 3.5 percent), but they would need to be structured in a way that the increases would be meaningful to the employee. You usually see this type of total rewards modification in the nursing industry and with IT professionals. The nursing profession, for example, is more nomadic, and by providing more frequent increases it might help slow down the movement.

A third thing organizations might do is create a separate salary structure for these hot-skills employees. Organizations have been using multiple salary structures for some time, however, in most cases this was for varying groups of employees within the organization (clerical, professional, managerial). By creating a separate structure for hot-skills employees, organizations will be better suited to accommodate any additional movement to the pay ranges for these employees.

Target Market Position

Most organizations tend to set pay targets at the 50th percentile. As discussed earlier, this means that most organizations tend to target pay at "what everyone else is paying." This may or may not work for all organizations. To attract qualified applicants for key positions within organizations, organizations may set pay targets higher than the 50th percentile. Some organizations might target the 75th percentile for key positions. This signifies that organizations recognize that several of their positions within them are key to the development and ongoing growth of the businesses. Therefore, those positions are more valuable and should have a higher pay target.

For example, in a retail environment the buyer position (the position that determines what goes into the stores and how much the stores should purchase) is an integral part of the business. A retail organization might want to attract the best buyers in the industry to ensure they have the exact product customers are looking for in an appropriate quantity. This organization might set pay targets higher than the 50th percentile to attract the best talent for the position.

Access to Salary Data

Now, more than ever, employees have access to free salary data, whether it is through the Internet, trade publications, newspapers or other sources. Therefore, it is important for compensation professionals to recognize that this information is available and employees are using it. Although this "free" data might not be the most accurate, it is important for an organization to at least review this information during compensation reviews and see how closely it matches the data that is normally used. Be sure to keep good documentation of the sources actually used and be prepared to address the reliability and validity of "free" sources.

SIDEBAR: Reliability of Today's Sources

- **Online sources** — It is important to know where the data is coming from, its source, and how old it is. This information will help determine how valid and reliable the data is. For example, if an online survey source uses two-year-old New York City salary data, then applies a governmentally available differential to apply that data to Phoenix, then applies an aging factor, the salary data information probably will not be very reliable. If the data source is city of Phoenix salary data from this year, then the reliability would be greater.
- **Trade publications** — With trade publications, it is very important to know the source of the data. A lot of times they might survey their audience to get the information. In this case, the data is not very reliable because the results cannot be validated. Did readers put a higher salary than they earn to inflate their worth when the survey came out?
- **Newspaper** — This is another source where it is very important to pay attention to the source and how the information is reported. Newspapers usually are looking for a "story," therefore, it is important to locate the source of the information and closely examine how the data is reported.

Performance Differentiation

In recent years, merit budgets have remained around the 3.5-percent range. Unfortunately, this becomes a problem when it is time to deliver merit increases to employees. It is very difficult to differentiate performance with such small budgets.

One way to address this issue is to use more variable pay. By using variable pay, managers will be able to make up for shortcomings by delivering a one-time lump sum. From an employee perspective they will receive the entire amount at one time, which is a plus. However, the monies will not be tied to base pay, which could be a negative.

Another way to address this is to inform managers that it is acceptable to give employees a zero (0) increase for the year if their performance does not justify an increase. This is very difficult for managers to understand, because compensation and merit increases, in particular, have become an entitlement for most employees. Throughout the years, organizations have not done a good job explaining that merit increases are based upon the "merits" of the employee, and comparatively speaking, if one or several employees are not performing, it is completely justifiable to give them a zero (0) increase.

It is important for organizations to determine a way to differentiate performers within the organization, and to ensure that high performers are being compensated.

As the compensation function continues to evolve within organizations (and as a profession), it is important for compensation practitioners to utilize the total rewards model to ensure the best talent is being attracted and retained. As new issues arise, understanding what employees value and how that value system influences employee engagement is a vital piece of the compensation function.

Articles & Perspectives

Compensation Philosophy: The Starting Point
By Christopher Kelley and David Gustat

Problem: *Your boss just let you know that the board of directors is really taking this corporate compliance thing seriously and has asked to have a recommendation on a new compensation philosophy at next month's board meeting. Your boss wants you to take the lead on developing the new compensation philosophy and presenting it to the board. The current compensation philosophy was developed 10 years ago, but nobody really knows much about the existing philosophy since it is rarely ever talked about.*

Start at the Beginning

Just what is a compensation philosophy anyway? What is it supposed to do? How should a compensation philosophy be developed?

Compensation philosophy may be best defined by what it is not. Compensation philosophy is not a be all, end all. Organizations don't develop a compensation philosophy and then forget about compensation completely. A compensation philosophy is the *starting point* for the journey through the land of compensation — not the destination. In addition, compensation philosophy is not simply a statement that proclaims, "We're a 50th-percentile payer." There's more to it than that. (See Sidebar 1 on page 83.)

In its simplest form a philosophy is a set of beliefs or principles that explains actions and practices. A philosophy answers the question, "Why?" In the context of compensation, it also answers the questions, "How do I set up every element of my compensation programs?" and "Which compensation programs make sense for my organization?" The principles outlined in a compensation philosophy should help any reader understand the following:

- Should pay be based on what competitors pay, or on internal worth?
- How should the organization be positioned relative to the market?

- Should pay be differentiated? If so, based on what? Performance? Knowledge? Seniority?
- Should pay be 100-percent fixed or should there should be a mix of base and variable?

Moreover, a sound compensation philosophy should have some connection to the overall strategy and mission of the company. To see this in action, let's look at two companies that both say they pay for performance in their compensation philosophy.

Company A: *As a manufacturer of high-margin widgets, Company A has a powerful, recognizable brand. Customers prefer its widgets to the competitors', even though they cost more. Company A makes the highest-quality product and charges more than its competition.*

This business philosophy translates to people, as well. The company hires the best, most qualified people, and pay them more than the competition — through their incentive plan. The pay plan is based on company sales performance, not individual performance. Incentive targets are set at competitive levels, but the maximum payout percentage is well above the competition. This translates into above-market incentive payouts when the business does well.

For Company A, pay for performance becomes "top pay for top company sales" and "average pay for average sales." Company A distinguishes individual performance through promotions and merit increases and therefore, offers more base pay.

Company B: *Company B manufactures inexpensive widgets. It spends less to make its widgets than the competition and passes that savings on to customers. Its brand is not recognizable by most consumers, but its widgets are usually the least expensive. Consumers know when they buy these widgets that they are sacrificing quality, but getting the best price. Company B hires good people, but loses many top candidates to the competition because minimizing costs also translates to minimizing salaries and the incentive plan. Incentive targets are set at competitive levels, but the maximum payout percentage is below competitive levels. The plan is based on overall company cost — the better the cost control, the better the payout.*

For Company B, pay for performance becomes "more pay for reduced costs."

Both Company A and Company B believe in pay for performance — but in different ways. Their industry and their basic strategies as to how they compete help determine their compensation philosophy. *A good compensation philosophy reflects the business philosophy.* Not the other way around. So which company has the "right" compensation philosophy? Maybe both. It really depends on how well the philosophy fits for each particular organization during each phase of the business life cycle.

By understanding the core ways the company competes and makes money, compensation professionals will begin to see a strategy. Many companies articulate this in a mission statement. But every company has a strategy, a way of doing business and a core set of beliefs. The job of the compensation professional is to ensure that the compensation philosophy reflects the business philosophy.

> **SIDEBAR 1: A "P50 Compensation Philosophy" is Not Enough**
>
> Many organizations have stated compensation philosophies to pay to the "50th percentile of the market." But this is far from adequate. It's important to have a target or a goal of where aggregated pay levels should fall relative to the labor market. However, a philosophy needs to address much more than that. Without articulating more about the beliefs about compensation, people in the organization are left to assume that everyone and every program simply needs to be at the 50th percentile.
>
> Executives and managers naturally think broader than a single statement of paying at the "50th percentile," but they're conditioned to think of a compensation philosophy that way. One way to break through that paradigm is to play the Actor Salary Survey game. Provide a listing of roughly 10 Hollywood actors and ask the executives to guess what the going rates are for each actor to have the lead role in a major motion picture.
>
> What's amazing is that in virtually every group where this exercise has been played, people always guess the pay levels with lots of variation. They know that some actors are worth more and some are worth less. Now ask executives to think about being a movie studio executive who follows a P50 pay philosophy. Offer a lead role to Tom Cruise for the 50th percentile and he'll likely hang-up the phone. Conversely, offer P50 to Edward Norton and he'll gladly accept, but then the executive would be fired for spending about $10 million more than necessary.
>
> The point of the exercise is to break the paradigm of being locked into a single number and appreciate that it is okay to pay what is appropriate. Use the market data as a guide. But exercise judgment, make good business decisions and understand the difference between an individual's pay and an overall positioning strategy against the market data.
>
> A well-articulated compensation philosophy may help employees throughout the organization understand the intentions and beliefs of the senior leaders. This improved understanding means that employees actually know/comprehend why certain programs are in place, which in turn leads to a more engaged workforce and a higher-performing organization.

How a Compensation Philosophy Works

A compensation philosophy is not just a sheet of paper expounding on how the company feels about different elements of compensation and how they are used. The philosophy is the starting point for all compensation design. Think of the compensation philosophy as the "moral compass" from which professionals set their direction for the compensation strategies and programs. It is the core from which individual compensation programs and strategies are built. The compensation philosophy should be the "stake in the ground" to which all compensation programs can be tied.

Organizations are frequently faced with having to evaluate new and emerging compensation programs. They also may need to assess the design of their annual incentive plans. With a solid compensation philosophy, the compensation or rewards professional's job becomes easier. New plans, or modifications to existing plans, should first be bounced against the philosophy to see if the changes fit the desired results.

Even without requests for changes or new plans, each company should proactively evaluate existing plans against existing philosophies to look for gaps in desired results. This will highlight possible needs for program changes to address these gaps.

How the Compensation Philosophy Is Developed

A compensation philosophy needs to be an expression of the beliefs of the most senior leadership in the organization. Ultimately, the board of directors has the ability to approve or reject the compensation philosophy and in some organizations, it may actually take an active role in defining it. The best compensation philosophies are those which are developed as part of a collaborative effort that involves and engages senior leadership members, but also takes into account as input the perspectives of a cross-section of other stakeholders in the organization. (See Sidebar 2 on page 85.)

Getting more perspectives takes more time. However, engaging the real stakeholders helps ensure buy-in down the road and might even help uncover any major disconnects between these critical players. Better to resolve these situations early, rather than have the differences boil over during the rollout of a program change.

> **SIDEBAR 2: Techniques for Developing an Effective Compensation Philosophy**
>
> The process for developing an effective compensation philosophy varies with each organization based on the culture for how decisions get made and the circumstances facing the organization. However, there are some common tips and techniques to consider when working with clients to help develop a compensation philosophy.
>
> **Senior leadership team:**
> - Be clear on the identity and role of the executive sponsor for developing/revising a compensation philosophy.
> - Engage the senior leadership team by conducting individual interviews.
> - Recap and gain consensus for the final compensation philosophy.
>
> **Cross-section of employee groups:**
> - If using employee groups for input, be sure to clearly communicate the purpose and expectations.
> - Use focus groups to gather rich, quality data. Use online surveys for more quantity, but less depth of info.
> - Gather information from top performers and ensure demographic representation.
>
> **External labor market:**
> - Research compensation philosophies of other similarly situated organizations.
> - In rare circumstances where attraction and retention are critical issues or trouble spots, consider surveying workers in external labor markets to identify values and desires.
>
> Boards all across America are faced with increasingly more scrutiny about the pay levels and practices in the corporations they represent, so it's not surprising that this project request may be given to the compensation department. With the thoughts and ideas presented here, compensation professionals are now better prepared to take on this challenge. And with some focused effort, they will be able to define the compensation philosophy that is right for their organizations.

About the Authors

Christopher Kelley is the managing partner at HR Analytic Services LLC. He can be reached at chris.kelley@hranalyticservices.com or 630/524-5818.

David Gustat is a consultant who focuses on providing strategic compensation solutions for organizations. He also serves as chairman of the WorldatWork Compensation Advisory Board. Gustat can be reached at dave@gustat.com.

Reprinted from *workspan* January 2006.

What Is Base Salary?
By Michael O'Malley, Ph.D.

Sometimes people do things that require reflection, as often their thoughts and actions are piloted in a direction that never breaks from a scripted logic or habitual course. Figuring and administering base salaries, at times, can be an exercise that is time-consuming, necessary and frequently automatic and rote.

Often, compensation professionals go through the motions, just trying to meet some end without considering the underlying rationale for their actions, such as when they use a hiring rate, a performance management form with measures and rating scale or a grade structure with progressions and ranges. Consistency surely is necessary, but sometimes it comes at the expense of true reflection and change.

The question, "What is base salary?" can startle compensation professionals who so often are caught up in the *doing*. Surprisingly, this simple question, which relates to one of the most fundamental business practices, can mysteriously stump scores of professionals. Despite the great energy spent in setting base salaries, many practitioners falter when they are asked to explain what they are trying to achieve and what salaries are they're intending to represent.

When an array of an organization's salaries is created, those dollar values embody implicit and explicit rules and meanings. They are an archive and rendering of past decisions. Among other things, they may signify the following:

- Market conditions
- The importance of a job to the company
- Employees' past and potential performances
- Prior experiences
- Hierarchical constraints (e.g., it is impossible to earn more than the boss)
- Tenure
- Skill sets
- Internal pressures to attract and retain talent.

Maintaining that base salary is all of these misses the point and is an admission that base salaries are, in essence, an amalgam of necessity and expedience; products of impromptu decisions and reactions, versus the outcome of sound, deliberate planning. The question, "What is base salary?" forces a revisiting to what is most important in determining base salary and, in relation, how best to fashion salary programs.

Creating a Definition
Step One
A healthy first step in salary planning is to stop and craft a definition for base salary: "Base salary in this organization represents …" What?

Limitless possibilities abound, which is why asking this basic question is so essential. Most companies make an assumption that salaries should denote the relative worth of an employee (his/her market value in the context of an organization's mission and culture) combined with some indicator, or set of indicators, of organizational value. These indicators usually — but not necessarily — are performance-related and should be specified. Performance can be construed as having two general dimensions:

- **Outcomes versus process (content).** Outcomes represent the tangible results of one's efforts: The fulfillment of goals, the meeting of expectations and the realization of accomplishments. Process refers to the enablers of those outcomes: The competencies, skills and abilities that are necessary ingredients for success.

- **Present versus future (time).** Present performance pertains to contemporary events, usually within the past year, or how a person has executed his/her job responsibilities in the current business-planning cycle. Future performance is the anticipatory value a person has on future assignments and job duties based on the qualities he/she possesses that may (or may not) be used in the current position. Sometimes, organizations ascribe future values to people who are designated as "high potential." There is a multitude of choices in how to attribute value.

An organization's approach to measurement should help underscore its claims (e.g., "superior compensation for superior results"). At the group level of measurement, this may imply that one company is better than all others on a set of select measures. At the individual level, this may imply that one employee is better than most others both inside and outside the organization on a set of select measures.

For example, the best researcher in a pharmaceutical company is not just someone who outshines his/her peers within the organization; it is someone who every other pharmaceutical company wants. "Superior" usually requires a reference to something or someone who is independent or outside of the system to which one belongs. A company's standards of excellence may not conform to others' conceptions of excellence.

Step Two

Secondly, base salary definitions should incorporate how practitioners arrive at indices of worth by explaining how the various relevant components will combine to affect base salaries. For example, it is insufficient to say only that base salaries mirror the market value of positions, results achieved, and skills and competencies expressed. It's necessary to describe the manner by which these elements blend together. Consider the three employees in Figure 1 and their respective scores on two hypothetical performance dimensions. All else being equal, who would you say should be paid the most relative to a market median?

With no basis or criteria from which to work, the answer is unclear; there is no understanding of base salary. Measures could be combined additively or multiplicatively, depending on how companies think about performance and, ultimately, how they care to reward people. Consider the following:

FIGURE 1: Which Employee Should Be Paid the Most Relative to a Market Median?

Employee	Performance Results	Performance Process
Employee 1	Rating = 4	Rating = 2
Employee 2	Rating = 3	Rating = 3
Employee 3	Rating = 2	Rating = 4

- If one practitioner believes that one type of performance augments another (as process surely may do for outcomes), then multiplicatively combining scores may be the prudent option.
- If another practitioner believes that base salaries reflect the sum total of an employee's performance — both process and results — then the scores are additively combined and the three employees are equal.
- If another practitioner weights the results three times more important than process, then Employee 1 would be the better performer.
- If yet another practitioner finds that base salaries reflect the joint effort of process and outcomes (i.e., performance is greater when employees possess both aspects in greater degrees), then Employee 2 would be the better performer (results multiplied by process).

Some organizations use what can be called a conditional definition of performance: They limit how high a manager, for example, can score on results based on how high he/she scores on process. The latter limits the former, reasoning that, "We will measure you on your results, but we will only count results up to a certain point depending on how well you perform on process." This measures performance on one's ability versus chance or other factors. In the example, if a results score can only be as high as a process score, Employee 2 again would win.

From Conception to Reality
After defining base salary and specifying how monetary values are assigned to employees, the employer needs to follow through on conception. The following three allocation rules, or a combination thereof, can be used to attach base salary amounts to people.

Equity
Equity is the familiar principle that "to each according to his/her contribution." The argument is that employees' salaries should be aligned with their performance in the way in which they are conceived: Past or present, process or outcome. The most common way of legislating equity has been through merit matrices. (Contrary to the rumor that this tool has died, matrices are alive and well and almost universally used in one form or another.)

Briefly, matrices view base salaries as a function of two components: Position in range and performance. Better performers who are the farthest below their midpoints receive the highest pay increases. Note: These systems recognize that base salaries are dynamic, and pure equity (performance-based distributions) is achievable only over time.

Also, it is critical to note that merit matrices or grids have their own embedded logic or assumptions. First, with standard grid systems, base salaries represent historical competence in one's position. That is, base salaries not only represent what people recently did, but what they have done in the past. The ostensive difference between a person well above midpoint versus one well below is not just this year's performance, but last year's, the prior year, etc. Secondly, current performances have different meanings depending on where people are within the salary range. For example, a given performance rating has greater implication for to base salary and greater incremental value for employees lower in the range versus those higher in the range.

There is nothing inherently right or wrong with these underlying assumptions, but they are, nonetheless, assumptions, and some companies find them palatable while others do not. Those that object typically believe that grids do not help create the meritocracy that is sought and cite two problems with achieving equity in this fashion:

- The divergence of dissimilar performers on pay for those below midpoint is too slow. (Higher performers do not readily break away from the pack due to resource constraints and other situational variables.)
- The convergence of dissimilar performers on pay for those above midpoint is too great. (As per the usual guidelines, mediocre to good employees begin to catch up with the truly superior employees.)

Essentially, some companies maintain that grids present too many contaminants to equity. Indeed, their suspicions are corroborated by studies that show the best predictors of base salaries are starting wage and time in the organization, with performance a sporadic and less influential contributor.

Most variations on a merit grid theme are attempts to refocus definition and meaning of base salary as a proxy for performance by correcting the purported defects. To bring salaries closer into alignment with true differences among employees, some companies take the following steps:

- **Insert time parameters.** Companies put time delimiters on how long it should take employees who display certain aptitudes and produce certain results to pass midpoint, usually shortening the period for the perennial superstars.
- **Broaden ranges or loosen the upper end of grids.** Companies allow greater discretion to continually move people who perform well up in salary.
- **Allocate separate merit pools.** Companies allocate more of their merit dollars to employees who are designated high performers (and less to others) so that differentiation between employees is speedier over time. This method often is used in tandem with procedures that restrict the number of high performers, more quickly widening the differences in pay among people who perform differently.
- **Use separate grid salary ranges for separate populations.** Companies carve up their salary ranges and apply the conventional grid to these various ranges for people who are low, medium and high performers, respectively. Essentially, they use higher midpoints for higher performers, permitting more rapid movement and faster monetary recognition of employees' contributions.

All of these approaches attempt to pay according to performance. To fulfill this aim, companies need to resist the habits of mechanistic application and ad hoc solutions.

Equality

Some companies consider person-related differences to be irrelevant to their base pay decisions. They take the time to collect and measure individual and specific items, such as performance, and provide feedback accordingly. But, when it comes to money, everyone is paid about the same by design. In this instance, the distributive rule is "to each equally," or "one for all and all for one." This may appear to be a simple rule with a simple application, but it is tricky in practice because the rule can be applied at any level of reward. For example, you can pay people equally and either well below or well above market. So, even in this instance, the whats and whys of base salary have to be determined.

As an example, consider a major chemical company that believes that everyone should be paid at the 75th percentile against their relevant set of comparator companies. Base salaries across the organization represent a particular market position, but several considerations go into this market placement (relative labor costs and affordability notwithstanding). The abilities to attract and retain talent, motivate employees and encourage collegiality all are viable concerns. This raises a broader issue about base salary: How to establish a definition and attendant actions that retain the intended functions of salaries. The concept of equity is attractive because, presumably, equity promotes motivation and, correspondingly, equality does not. This is another common assumption that mostly goes unchallenged.

As it happens, evenly high salaries in concert with other HR programs (e.g., performance feedback) may facilitate motivation and other positive behaviors. Research shows that, as people's salaries increase, they become less concerned with relative pay proportionate to their contributions. That is, if you treat everyone especially well, they are less vigilant about how others fare in the pay system. Also, evidence suggests that high pay stimulates positive employee attitudes and citizenship and encourages greater effort (aka, "the overjustification effect" or, high pay acts as an inducement to try harder). The overriding point is that compensation professionals sometimes are dismissive of potential base salary programs because of an errant belief system.

Need

At the programmatic level, dollar allocations based on need usually resemble equality, with salaries uniformly set at median market levels and annual adjustments made according to the cost of living. Base salary's purpose is to provide sustenance; to make sure that people have enough. These systems typically are found in large, privately held companies in which cultures of paternalism tend to prevail.

The problem with need-based base salary programs is that ultimately, needs are personal and idiosyncratic. Using base salaries to respond to employees' economic situations or shortfalls (e.g., marriages, birth of children, prolonged periods of tepid pay increases, etc.) yields programs that are counterintuitive. Promotions and raises are made without due consideration to other things that matter. People are paid for responsibilities that they cannot fulfill and life choices to which not everyone subscribes. Nevertheless, it is conceivable to develop salary programs founded on need, and some companies literally make pay decisions on these grounds.

You Have to Pay What You Have to Pay — Or Do You?

What does the core definition of base salary encompass and exclude? Most companies create policies that attempt to handle anomalies and preserve the core meaning of "base salaries." Usually, this involves specifying what you will handle through base salaries and what is best left to the other varieties of rewards and HR devices.

For example, you may believe that years of service is an important corporate quality, but one that you prefer to recognize with a gold watch as opposed to ramped-up wages. Similarly, frantic managerial appeals for higher salaries to retain employees may be handled through other means (e.g., variable compensation, new and energizing job assignments, car allowances, etc.).

Perhaps you may decide to impose dollar limits on new-hire salaries if paying the amounts required to attract a candidate would exceed a level of salary that is tolerable, and instead treat the difference with sign-on bonuses or stock. Without a strong foundation and resolve for what constitutes base salary, the keepers of the salary system will be mercilessly subject to a free-for-all for dollars with a resulting program that makes little sense.

The expression, "You have to pay what you have to pay" suggests that whatever you pay, regardless of cost, is always right. If it's necessary, then it must be correct, right? Wrong. Pay programs that strive for this so-called flexibility typically do not have order and seldom are regarded as fair by employee beneficiaries.

For example, Sally is a soft-spoken, solid citizen and performer who quietly takes what she is given, which is less than she deserves; hot shot Mark was hired at a ridiculous premium; Deirdre's pot was sweetened when she threatened to quit; Tom's salary was enhanced following the successful completion of an important project — as a kind of thank-you; Bart, who is a decent performer, hasn't gotten a raise in two years because of his misfortune of working in an underachieving division; Lionel has been with the company forever and has profited through the cumulative effects of time.

Not that these things don't happen, or even that they shouldn't. But in the tough and often-thankless world of the compensation manager, someone should have the discipline and assertion to produce a plan that underscores which considerations will be included and not included in salaries.

We sometimes think that we are doing a pretty good job at managing salaries when, upon analyzing our pay dispersions, we discover that most employees fall within a competitive range. We have seen these results produce a modicum of comfort. In truth, it isn't that hard to pay people within a competitive range. The margins are relatively wide ($36,000 to $54,000 for a position with a $45,000 midpoint), and those at the fringes either take care of themselves (people below or near minimums never join the organization or self-select out) or are taken care of (those near or above the maximums are promoted, retired or let go).

Simple omnibus comparisons to the market do not prove that a salary system is working. When an employee asks, "What is base salary, anyway?" you should have a ready answer with evidence to attest to the validity of your assertion. Base salaries should be revealing of the organization's core factors and principles.

The proof is in the demonstration that observed distinctions in salaries are legitimate. Are actual salaries explainable, or predictable, from the information used to generate them? (Statistical methods can answer this question.) The results of your query show how far the company's base wages depart from your stated intentions and the extent to which extraneous factors were permitted to encroach on your program. Competitive analyses of your pay practices ought not simply be an exercise in determining how you measure up to market, but ought to offer a pragmatic and rigorous way of examining the logic of your salary program and its susceptibility to capriciousness.

About the Author

Michael O'Malley, Ph.D., is a vice president and practice leader in the New York office of Clark/Bardes Consulting. He has more than 20 years of human resources consulting experience, with areas of specialization in compensation design, organization development and research, and leadership. O'Malley is the best-selling author of *Are You Paid What You're Worth?* and *Creating Commitment*. He has been the featured guest on more than 100 radio and television broadcasts and is a frequent keynote speaker at national conferences and executive retreats.

O'Malley has a bachelor's degree from Case Western Reserve University, where he was selected Phi Beta Kappa. He has his doctorate in social psychology from Vanderbilt University. He is a member of the American Psychological Association and the Society for Industrial and Organizational Psychologists. O'Malley is the winner of both the Stephen Bednarik and Richard Griffith Memorial awards for achievements in the field of psychology.

Reprinted from *WorldatWork Journal* Third Quarter 2003.

Market Pricing 101: The Science and the Art
By Deb Grigson, John Delaney and Robert Jones, JD, CPA, CEBS

Whether you are a seasoned veteran who market prices 2,000 jobs a year or you are newly charged with converting your company's 20-year-old point system to a market-based pay system, the world of salary surveys — just like the stock market — is ever changing. Staying abreast of new developments will keep you ready and able to meet the challenges placed on you as your company's market-pay expert.

The effort to balance current payroll against the market is critical because of the need to hire, retain and properly motivate the best people. Really, the market is the backdrop behind which a company's show is created. In this Web-access world, one can assume that every employee has a fairly good idea of how much his or her co-workers earn in terms of base salary. Using market data effectively helps the business logically and consistently present its market-pay position to employees. While an employer's market position is important, the consistency with which market data is collected — and the consistency in creating supporting pay polices around that market — is what creates an atmosphere of employee commitment.

Step One: Buy the Right Data
There are many surveys from many different sources available every year. Selecting the right survey sources is predicated on a good understanding of the business and how it relates to the market. To start, there are a few questions that need to be answered:

- From which market do I hire employees?
- To what market am I losing employees?
- In which market would my company *like* to compete?

The answers to these questions will create a description of a company's market position and lead to the survey sources that provide data relevant to a specific market. You may find that different job groups have different markets. If so, then different survey sources are needed for different employee populations or, at the very least, a survey that has the data cut (i.e., the way a particular vendor separates data, such as by geographic location, number of employees or market segment) the company requires. (See "Market Comparators" on page 101.)

After determining the market your company competes in (or the one it wants to compete in based on its job groups), it's time to select the surveys. Survey vendors will willingly review the participant and job list available in their surveys. Clearly describe to the vendor the market comparisons that best represent the business, then determine how many of your company's positions are represented in the selected survey's job list. It is relatively easy to find surveys for jobs that are common to many industries (e.g., administrative assistant), and a good all-around survey will have most of these jobs available.

But it may become more challenging to find survey sources when looking for executive jobs, unique industry jobs and/or sales jobs. But there are resources, such as *Survey Sources for U.S. and International Employee Pay and Benefits,* published by Personnel Systems Associates, that can help focus the search. While the cost may be more per useful market data point due to the specialized nature of the data, it may be worth the money because it's the only way to obtain the necessary data.

Surveys come in all price ranges and many formats beyond the traditional paper reports. PDFs and electronic and Web-based tools provide flexibility that was not practical just a few years ago. Choose the format that works best for the company. Depending on the number of pricings you expect to conduct annually, one system may be more cost-effective than another. Many vendors (e.g., Radford, McLagan, etc.) maintain compensation Web sites that allow users to review the qualification of the survey, costs and methods for delivery.

Light users (i.e., fewer than 50 jobs annually with minimal analytic requirements) will find that buying a printed or PDF report is sufficient, as data can be manipulated via in-house spreadsheets. "Power" users (i.e., more than 50 jobs annually with or without fairly extensive analytic requirements) will find electronic versions more easily manipulated and shared among stakeholders.

Power users should consider some form of Web-based market-pricing tool that enhances the use of the electronic data and facilitates the process of creating composite pricings (multiple survey jobs and sources). These tools will cut in half the time commitment for market pricing and even survey submission. Plan how much administration is necessary for the market-pricing effort, and then make sure you have the surveys and systems to meet the demand.

Club, Industry-Specific and Local Surveys: Gold

Surveys come in all shapes and sizes. Many companies participate in and subscribe to club, industry-specific or local surveys.

- **Club Surveys.** Provided via a professional organization. Participating in and receiving data from the club survey is a privilege of membership. Local and industry-specific surveys can be club surveys. These surveys are chosen when they closely represent a company's market position and the data cannot be found more economically elsewhere.

- **Local Surveys.** Often provide a number of general-industry entry-level positions. To find local survey data, check with local HR organizations to see if they can provide the name of a local survey provider.
- **Industry-Specific Surveys.** Usually provided via a professional organization specific to the business.

For a survey to be useful, the participant list, survey jobs and specific data cuts must be relevant to the company's established market position. Evaluate the quality of the data before committing to a purchase. Review the provider's methodology section. Many of the following facts will be described in the methodology section:

- Number of participants
- Data collection period
- Excluded data and reasons
- Positions included
- Type of data cuts available, industries, geographies, etc.
- Information about the survey vendor.

If you choose to buy a club survey, you may have an opportunity to participate in creating the survey jobs and methodology for data collection and analysis. This is a good opportunity to ensure that the survey provides your company with the positions and data you need most. Note of caution: The survey jobs should always be generic enough to ensure comfortable matching by selected businesses outside of your own.

Custom Surveys

Despite the array of surveys available, there are many underrepresented niche positions or industries. Custom surveys can help define these hard-to-reach markets, and can answer unique, qualitative questions (e.g., the frequency of the incentive payout). If you choose to conduct a custom survey, choose a partner with experience collecting and analyzing compensation data. Current laws and trends in governance strongly suggest that a "disinterested" third party conduct salary surveys. A good partner also will ensure that each survey question is designed to elicit the quantity and quality of answers most useful to you, the survey sponsor. Custom surveys can be conducted either using your company's name as the source or anonymously. Typically, all participants receive the results in exchange for participation.

Step Two: Defensible Market Pricing

After developing the market position and selecting the surveys, it's time to begin the market-pricing task. Collect job codes, titles, families and descriptions for the jobs being market priced. Also collect the following:

- Incumbent data
- Unique identifiers
- Base pay data
- Bonus pay data
- Long-term incentive data
- Demographic data (e.g., department, location, budget code, etc.)

Ensure the HRIS request has any possible "cuts" of data you may want to use to analyze positions against the market. Experts agree that jobs should be priced based on job content alone.

Next, organize position data up front. Think through how the company will want to compare the data (e.g., by business unit, budget code, department, job functions and families, etc.).

Position Matching

Select a family of jobs to price, then organize the jobs by their natural hierarchy. Select the job at the bottom or the top of the hierarchy and match that job first. This will establish an anchor job.

Job matching is the process by which a company's jobs are matched to a survey's jobs. Many survey vendors offer job-matching conferences. These provide excellent opportunities to validate the matching exercise and ensure that you are using the same measuring stick as other compensation experts.

To get started, read your job documentation and note the facts about the following:

- What the job does
- How much experience is necessary to do the job
- Who the job reports to
- Whether the position is supervisory
- The extent to which the successful completion of the job's content affects the company's overall success.

This process is called leveling. It is important to understand the level of the company position and the level of the positions documented by the survey. Generally, they are not the same.

The importance of job matching cannot be overstated. It is important to carefully choose matches and document the reasons for selecting each match; clients and business leaders will challenge the matches. If there are questions about the job responsibilities for an in-house job, call the supervisor and review the responsibilities. If there are questions regarding the vendor's survey job description, call the vendor for clarification. After selecting the job match and level, it's time to select the data cut.

Selecting a Data Cut

This goes back to the very first step. When you considered potential survey sources, you also considered how to best describe the market. Selected data cuts should follow your market (i.e., if you determined that the company is a pharmaceutical firm with revenues of $1.5 billion and those options exist in the survey, the data cut is an accurate reflection of the company's market position).

Note of caution: It is important to be consistent throughout the process to create credibility. The surveys and data-cut selections should always be consistent. If you cannot find adequate representation for your chosen market, then drop the qualification that makes the choice too narrow. In the case of the $1.5-billion pharmaceutical company that employs 500 people, the qualification to cut likely is the number of employees. After making the decision to broaden the scope of your search, stick with that search for the remainder of the market pricings. Some matches may have to be dropped because they do not have the exact market comparators. This is expected, and you will have a more defensible analysis when providing the business with an apples-to-apples study.

After determining that the survey job and the company job are a good, defensible match, the next step is to determine the quality of data. General parameters include the following:

- **Number of Companies in the Match.** Data is less reliable with fewer companies. Usually, surveys will not report less than five company matches. Typically, five company matches offer the best opportunity for a decent data range.
- **Number of Incumbents in the Match.** Data is less reliable with fewer incumbents. Some jobs can be expected to be one company and one incumbent, but you should only accept these ratios when it makes sense based on your understanding of the job content.
- **This Year's Data vs. Last Year's Data.** Note: This requires two years of data. A data analysis can be conducted to see if the trend is reasonable, but the definition of "reasonable" is variable — it depends on the market. Consider the technology industry as an example. In the past two years this segment's salary data has slowed considerably, and there are no expectations that the data will move much up or down. If there is a jump in the data, some investigation is necessary to determine where the data is coming from and whether there has been a change in quantity or quality of data providers.

If after close examination you do not feel the data is good, throw it out. Remember: Using bad data erodes your professional credibility and the company's ability to rely on the market.

Data Adjustments

What if the match is pretty good, but not perfect? Vendors place the most important job responsibilities in the first sentence of the position description. Based on this parameter, try to achieve at least an 80-percent match. A plus or minus 20-percent adjustment (i.e., a job content adjustment) is fine, provided the survey data does not have a better match and you are reasonably content with the match. To defend your position, document your reason for creating an adjustment to the data point. Not only will the documentation help defend the market position, it will help re-create your work next year — long after you've forgotten when you chose this path in the first place.

Other adjustments can be made, as well, and should represent the position match and the company's market position. The following adjustments are common:

- Aging the data
- Making geographic adjustments
- Leading or lagging the market.

Data should be aged consistently. Vendors collect market data as of a specific effective date. That data can be aged to today or to some time in the future. Every survey source can have a different effective date, so the apples-to-apples rationale applies. Remember: Pick one date and stick with it.

The first question to consider is how much to age the data. One option is to age all data to the market's reported annual change rate, which is found in the pay-practices section of the selected surveys and/or in one of the merit-increase and salary-structure annual surveys. Many companies will pick one aging percent (e.g., 4 percent) and stick to it across company jobs, surveys and various measures (i.e., base pay, bonus pay, long-term incentives). A case can be made for variability; for example, officer positions versus all others. Often these populations have different aging rates. A case can be made for a different aging percentage for base salary and variable pay. Again, if the market supports it and it can be used consistently, it could be a valuable tool for creating your defensible position in the market.

Geographic adjustments usually are made to data points when the position is hired locally, but the data is collected nationally. Take, for example, the position of administrative assistant. If you collect national data for the position but need to attract and retain in Manhattan, you will find that you need to make an adjustment to the original data to ensure a competitive rate. Geographic adjustments typically are applied to the market pricing one it is complete.

Finally, a company may choose to lead or lag the market in a particular sector or job group to reflect a business position. If a company has a group of jobs that are key to the business, it would be effective to lead the market. In this case, consider adjusting the market data position by some agreeable percentage to reflect the company's commitment to the position.

Survey Composites

The use of three or more survey sources is recommended. Remember: Despite a vendor's best efforts, levels of organization participation change annually. As such, there will be some variability in every survey source. Using several different sources creates less variability for pricings just by creating a bigger data pool. The market pricing that results from the combination of several survey sources is called a composite. Composites can be created in several ways:

- Simple average of the data points
- Employee-weighted (the weighted average based on all reported employee data points, when the survey vendor provides data this way)
- Company-weighted (the weighted average based on the number of companies providing aggregate data, when the survey vendor provides data this way).

Difficult-to-Match Jobs

Most companies have a number of jobs that are not easy to match. This typically requires a bit of creativity. Sometimes the position is a combination of jobs that can be matched independently; for example, the manager of housekeeping and the manager of engineering. If one incumbent holds both jobs, then a blended approach may be the best way to go. There are a couple of questions that can help guide this process:

- What percent of time does the incumbent perform duties for Job A? Job B?
- Are the skills, experience and/or education more or less for one of the jobs?

Based on your answers, you can apply a relative weight to the two jobs and combine them 50/50, 80/20 or whatever the case may be.

Another technique is to match the job to a matched internal job, then apply an adjustment factor of 5 percent to 15 percent. If the adjustment is up, it is called a premium. If the adjustment is down, it is called a discount. This technique indicates that the two jobs are similar in content, but one is bigger or smaller than the matched internal job.

When making adjustments and allowances, document the work. As stated, this adds credibility to the pricing and it sets you up for successfully re-creating the work next year.

Benchmarking

Benchmarking is the practice of choosing a sample of the total number of jobs in the company for the market-pricing analysis. This is usually done when it is not necessary or economical to market price all positions in a company. A few tips for successful benchmarking include the following:

- Try to price 30 percent to 50 percent of the jobs.
- Select jobs from each job grouping.
- Include jobs that are common to many companies and can be reliably found in the survey data, along with a few jobs that you think will be hard-to-find positions.

As a starting point, try to use a first-level job and the highest executive job in the study, along with selected positions in that range. This will help frame all positions and ensure they are appropriately anchored in the market. The jobs that you do not market price will need to be "slotted" into the organizational hierarchy after you are satisfied with the benchmarked market-pricing results.

> **SIDEBAR: Market Comparators**
>
> Surveys and survey data typically represent a variety of market comparators, including the following:
> - All data
> - Revenue size
> - Profitability
> - Geography
> - Industry
> - Employee count
> - Organization type (e.g., nonprofit/profit)
> - Budget
> - Specific peer group comparisons
> - Net income

Successful Market Pricing

Upon completion, check pricings against the current incumbent average, job by job. When the market and current incumbent pay levels are markedly different, experienced market analysts evaluate the company's documentation, then the incumbent's history and contributions to determine the reason for the mismatch. It may be that the job is undervalued or overvalued, or perhaps the job documentation is inaccurate. Every aspect of the job should be analyzed to ensure accurate matches. This is the cornerstone of the market-pricing process. Once the process is complete, you are ready to start using your data to analyze your company's position against the market.

About the Authors

Deb Grigson is an assistant vice president with Aon Consulting and has been a WorldatWork member since 1998.

John Delaney is a senior consultant with Aon Consulting and has been a WorldatWork member since 2002.

Bob Jones, JD, CPA, CEBS, is a senior vice president and regional practice leader of the Northeast Region for Compensation for Aon Consulting and has been a WorldatWork member since 1997. They can be reached at 610/834-2100.

Reprinted from *workspan* October 2004.

Linking Compensation Policies and Programs to Organizational Effectiveness

By Dow Scott, Ph.D., Richard S. Sperling, CCP, Thomas D. McMullen and Marc Wallace

There is little agreement on which pay philosophies are best in any given situation. With the exception of executive compensation, few empirical studies attempt to link compensation policies and programs to organizational effectiveness. Lack of empirical evidence, however, has not prevented compensation managers, academicians and consultants from prescribing a variety of policies and programs aimed at providing organizations with a competitive advantage. Since labor represents a major cost of operating a business, it would be in the managers' best interests to learn which pay policies and programs are most prevalent in successful organizations.

Consequently, recent research tried to determine which base pay compensation programs are most commonly used in organizations today, and if a relationship exists between compensation programs and organizational effectiveness.

Research Methods

Identifying the Research Population

The goal of the first phase of the study was to identify the pay policies and practices organizations are using today by reviewing literature and interviewing academics, consultants and practitioners. The research team drew heavily upon its more than 80 years of combined experience in the compensation field. Differences in terminology and program definitions used in the compensation field created a significant challenge to the research. To meet this challenge, the team tried to find the most common or universally used terminology and to provide definitions for policies or programs to minimize confusion for respondents.

The team also recognized that there are variations in pay policies and programs across different organizational levels and occupations within the same organization. For example, exempt and nonexempt employees within the United States often are paid very differently. Consequently, research focused on managerial and professional employees since most organizations tend to have a uniform set of policies and practices for this group. The senior executive team was excluded from the study because its pay policies and practices often are unique. Furthermore, compensation managers would have substantial knowledge of the policies and programs for professional and managerial employees, especially since they are probably included in this group for pay purposes. Finally, this employee group tends to have a significant impact on total organizational performance, making this a critical group to understand in terms of pay policies and programs and organizational effectiveness.

Developing the Survey Instrument

In Phase 2, the team constructed a data-collection instrument with statements and response categories that would generate a set of standardized responses so the data could be quantitatively analyzed. To enhance the richness of the findings, open-ended items were included to ensure that nonstandardized responses were captured. During Phase 2, there were three cycles of pilot tests with compensation managers, consultants and academicians before the survey instrument was finalized.

The final version of the survey instrument asked participants to describe and evaluate their managerial and professional pay policies and programs as they related to the following:

- Compensation philosophy and goals
- Methods of valuing work
- Base salary structure and design
- Pay administration and communication.

The study did not examine incentive pay programs because a lengthened survey might have discouraged compensation managers from responding. A second study is in progress that will examine the relationship between incentive pay plans and organizational effectiveness.

Defining 'Successful'

Three measures determined the effectiveness of the pay policies and programs. First, the team compared the pay policies and programs between companies that received *Fortune* magazine's 2002 "America's Most Admired Company" designation for their industry sector and those that did not receive that designation. *Fortune's* "Most Admired Companies" is a highly regarded annual survey of corporate reputations of more than 10,000 executives, directors and analysts. Conducted by Hay Group, the survey invites them to rate companies, overall and within industry groupings, on criteria ranging from financial soundness and use of corporate assets to quality of management and quality of products and services.

Second, the team collected 2002 total shareholder return (TSR) information for the publicly traded companies that responded to this survey. TSR is defined as the monthly percentage growth in stock price and dividends paid over the five-year period. The team divided the TSR data into quartiles and compared survey responses for the highest TSR quartile (i.e., the top 25 percent of companies) with data from companies in the lowest or bottom quartile of TSR (i.e., the lowest 25 percent of the companies).

Finally, survey respondents were asked to make a personal assessment of the effectiveness of their compensation policies and practices. Although this measure may be subjective, a compensation manager's perception of the degree of program effectiveness is a reliable indicator of success.

Response Rate

More than 9,000 WorldatWork members were invited to complete the survey. The membership sample targeted the highest-level compensation manager for each company. The survey was posted on the WorldatWork Web site for two weeks prior to the December 2002 holiday season. An e-mail communication was sent to each compensation manager from the sample requesting that the selected compensation managers access the Web site and complete the survey. There were 1,226 responses — a 12-percent response rate. Typical response rates are usually well below 10 percent. Over 99 percent of respondents completed the entire survey and were included in the analysis. Figures 1, 2 and 3 on pages 104 and 105 show how the sample represented virtually all industries and organization sizes.

The analyses reported here are descriptive statistics and t-tests comparing responses between "Most Admired" and other companies, and comparing companies with the highest TSR (i.e., top quartile) and those with the lowest TSR (i.e., bottom quartile). Findings are examined in three sections:

- Pay communication and employee understanding of the pay programs
- Direct compensation policies and practices
- Methods companies used to value work.

Pay Communication and Employee Understanding

Limited information is communicated about pay programs to managerial and professional employees. When asked how much information was shared with employees about their pay, respondents indicated the following:

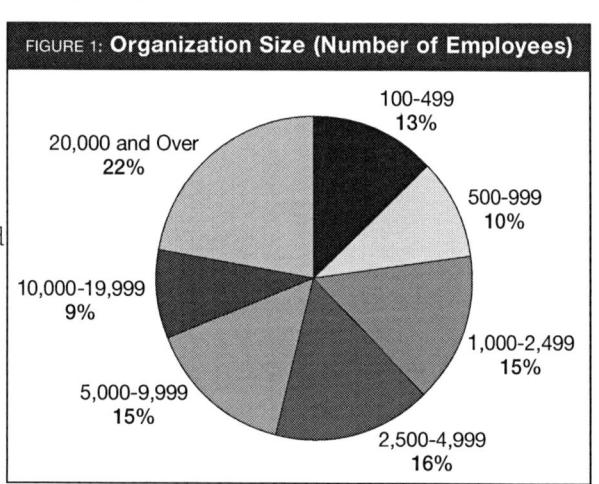

FIGURE 1: **Organization Size (Number of Employees)**

- 100-499: 13%
- 500-999: 10%
- 1,000-2,499: 15%
- 2,500-4,999: 16%
- 5,000-9,999: 15%
- 10,000-19,999: 9%
- 20,000 and Over: 22%

- 23 percent provided minimal information.
- 59 percent provided information regarding the design of the pay program.
- 7 percent provided the base salary for the employee's pay grade.
- 23 percent provided base salary ranges for all pay grades or jobs.
- 3 percent provided actual pay levels for all employees.

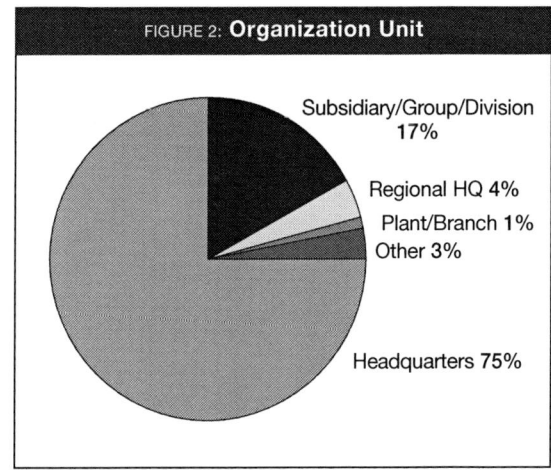

FIGURE 2: **Organization Unit**

Subsidiary/Group/Division 17%
Regional HQ 4%
Plant/Branch 1%
Other 3%
Headquarters 75%

Organizations used a variety of channels to communicate the pay program, with a heavy reliance on communications through management, including the following:

- 86 percent communicate via individual discussions with a supervisor.
- 54 percent utilize individual discussions with the HR or compensation department.
- 41 percent communicate via e-mails and memos.
- 34 percent communicate via employee meetings.
- 31 percent post information on the company Web site.
- 2 percent never communicate.

The frequency of pay communication is low, with 52 percent of the respondents indicating that they only communicate with employees once a year, 35 percent two or three times a year and 10 percent four to six times a year. There were no substantial differences in how employers

FIGURE 3: **Industry**

	Number of Respondents	Percent (May not add to 100 due to rounding)
Manufacturing	225	19%
Health care	144	12%
High Tech	118	10%
Finance/Banking	106	9%
Wholesale/Retail Trade	82	7%
Insurance	69	6%
Business Services	46	4%
Utilities	40	3%
Communications	40	3%
Service – Nonprofit	34	3%
Transportation	28	2%
Oil/Gas/Natural Resources	26	2%
Construction/Real Estate	19	2%
Government	16	1%
Education Services	15	1%
Publishing/Newspaper	11	1%
Other	156	13%

communicate to employees across different levels of TSR and companies that either held or did not hold "Most Admired" designations.

More than two-thirds (68 percent) of respondents evaluated their pay communications to be not effective or marginally effective. Interestingly, companies identified as "Most Admired" or those in the top quartile of total shareholder return (TSR) did not evaluate their communications any more positively than the companies that were rated less effective. However, a more in-depth examination of how pay philosophy information is communicated reveals differences between effective and less effective companies.

Ninety-one percent of respondents indicated that their company had a compensation philosophy. However, only 62 percent of these compensation managers said their philosophy was documented. Articulating the pay philosophy in writing was a distinguishing characteristic of "Most Admired" companies and those companies with the highest TSR. (See Figure 4.) A written philosophy indicates senior management understands and is committed to aligning its business strategy with pay, suggesting that alignment can have a positive impact on organizational effectiveness.

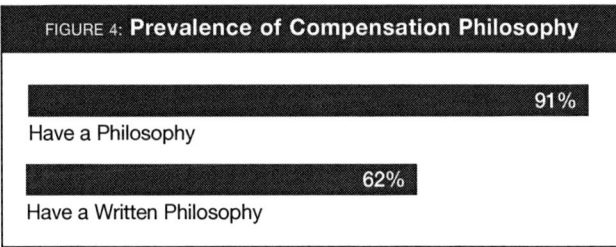

A documented philosophy also may be interpreted as evidence that management is attempting to communicate its business and compensation strategies to employees. If a written compensation policy facilitates communication of the business strategy, employees may respond to this message by working more effectively. As might be expected, survey results indicate that employees are more likely to understand their company's pay philosophy when it is documented than when it's not documented.

Base Pay

Compensation managers overwhelmingly reported that base salaries and total cash were positioned at the middle of the market. Over 80 percent of respondents said their goal for base pay for managerial and professional employees was the 40th and 60th percentile, and, in fact, 72 percent believed that their actual pay levels were at or near median. (See Figure 5 on page 107.) Although statistically it is impossible for everyone to be median, compensation managers may either be targeting different labor markets or considering such a large variety of jobs that they covered most of the overall pay distribution.

Most pay ranges for managers and professional employees were less than 70 percent wide. There was no discernable difference in range width between companies in the top quartile of TSR and those companies not providing that level of return. Unlike what the compensation literature implies, the survey data indicates that few companies have implemented "broadbanding" for their professional and managerial employees.

When asked how base salary increases were determined for managerial and professional employees, the following was reported:

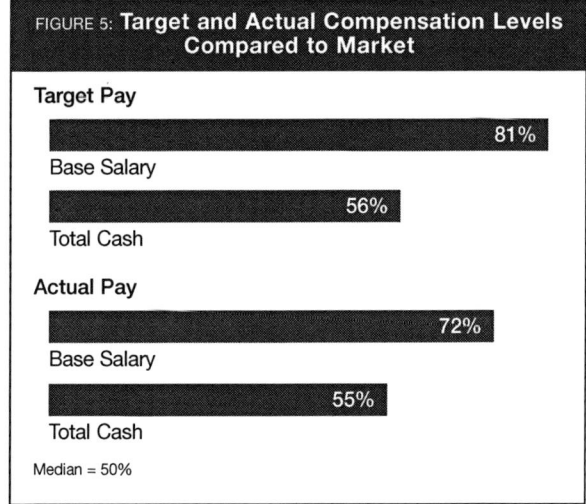

FIGURE 5: **Target and Actual Compensation Levels Compared to Market**

Target Pay
- Base Salary: 81%
- Total Cash: 56%

Actual Pay
- Base Salary: 72%
- Total Cash: 55%

Median = 50%

- 68 percent said that individual performance was compared to job standards.
- 50 percent compared performance to pre-established objectives or MBOs.
- 50 percent used the market value of the position.
- 22 percent judged performance on skill or competency acquisition.
- 9 percent based increases on years of service.
- 8 percent gave general increases to everyone.

These data indicate that most pay increases are based on individual merit, such as performance, compared to job standards, competency acquisition or MBOs. Less than 10 percent of respondents indicated that their organizations used years of service or general increases. However, 50 percent said they would give pay increases based on the job value in the marketplace. This represents a major change in how pay-increase budgets are used today compared to even five years ago. This change may be because merit budgets have been modest in recent years and increases have not been substantial enough to move employees with good performance records toward the top of the range. Nearly one-third (33 percent) of the respondents indicated that their performance-rating system does not, at least directly, drive pay increases. This is a significant minority given the current emphasis on pay for performance.

Variation in pay increases between high and average performers was surprisingly narrow. Almost one-third (32 percent) of respondents said that pay increases were more than double the increases given to average employees. Although the idea that top employees should be highly rewarded, even during economically difficult times, has received considerable press, this does not seem to be occurring in most organizations.

Survey findings indicated that base pay structures are adjusted annually (74 percent); market pricing or pay surveys are conducted annually (60 percent); and most salary ranges are less than 70 percent (72 percent).

When asked which performance measures senior management use to judge pay-program effectiveness, more than two-thirds (69 percent) said "employee turnover or retention." (See Figure 6.) The second most common evaluation criterion was through employee satisfaction surveys (40 percent). Business operating results and employee productivity were likely not reported as being used as frequently as evaluation criteria since the study focused on base pay and not incentive pay. Interestingly, companies designated as "Most Admired" and top TSR were more likely to use employee retention as primary criterion for evaluating the effectiveness of their pay systems than other surveyed companies. (See Figure 7.) This is a clear indicator of how successful organizations view base pay.

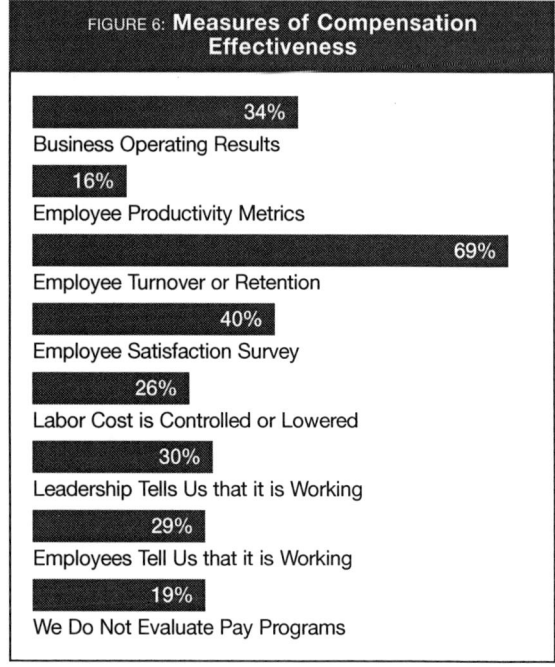

FIGURE 6: **Measures of Compensation Effectiveness**

- 34% Business Operating Results
- 16% Employee Productivity Metrics
- 69% Employee Turnover or Retention
- 40% Employee Satisfaction Survey
- 26% Labor Cost is Controlled or Lowered
- 30% Leadership Tells Us that it is Working
- 29% Employees Tell Us that it is Working
- 19% We Do Not Evaluate Pay Programs

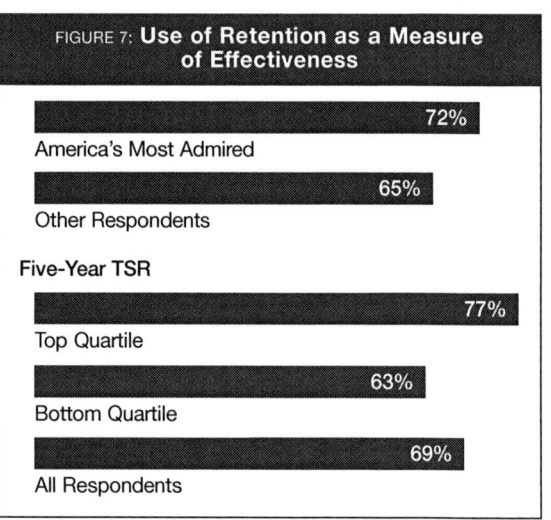

FIGURE 7: **Use of Retention as a Measure of Effectiveness**

- 72% America's Most Admired
- 65% Other Respondents

Five-Year TSR
- 77% Top Quartile
- 63% Bottom Quartile
- 69% All Respondents

Valuing Work

A substantial majority (between 82 percent and 96 percent) of compensation managers indicated that they used some form of job evaluation, and 98 percent of organizations market price their jobs (i.e., conducted pay surveys). In fact, the vast majority of organizations do both — up to 93 percent of organizations evaluate and market price jobs. This finding demonstrates that some of the HR discussions regarding the debate on the appropriateness between job evaluation and market pricing are essentially moot, at least for professional and managerial employees. Thus, it seems that most compensation professionals recognize that both job evaluation and market pricing are critical, and engage in both processes.

There are no clear patterns, however, in how organizations resolve conflicts between market pricing and job evaluation information. When there are conflicts between the job evaluation and market data, 38 percent of compensation managers give priority to job evaluation and the same percentage give priority to market pricing. Eleven percent of the respondents combine the two approaches, relying on job evaluation to set the job grade or level and market pricing to set pay levels.

Ninety-seven percent of survey respondents reported that their organization has some form of job documentation, but only 32 percent said that they had up-to-date job descriptions on almost all (over 90 percent) of their jobs. Thirty-four percent reported that most job descriptions are not up-to-date. This is a serious problem not only for organizations that use job evaluation, but also for those that use market pricing since the accuracy of these tools depends to a degree on having an up-to-date understanding of the work, which in many cases is obtained via job descriptions.

While there has been much talk of line management taking a stronger role in valuing work and making pay decisions, HR managers are primarily accountable for this process. In 60 percent of the surveyed companies, HR alone assigned jobs to grades. HR and line managers collaborated on the job evaluation process in only 28 percent of the surveyed companies. Successful companies were even more likely to have HR alone assign jobs to a salary grade. (See Figure 8.) In addition, 60 percent of organizations indicated that job grades are reviewed only in response to a request from managers or incumbents. Only 18 percent of organizations proactively review or audit job grades periodically.

Given the overall context created by out-of-date job descriptions, limited involvement of line management and reactive review of job grades, it was not surprising to find that 41 percent of survey participants believe that at least 20 percent of their organization's jobs are placed in the wrong grades. There are serious cost implications for assigning jobs to the wrong grade. For example, if 20 percent of a company's positions are in an incorrect grade, and grades typically are 10 percent apart, then

FIGURE 8: Role of HR in Work Evaluation

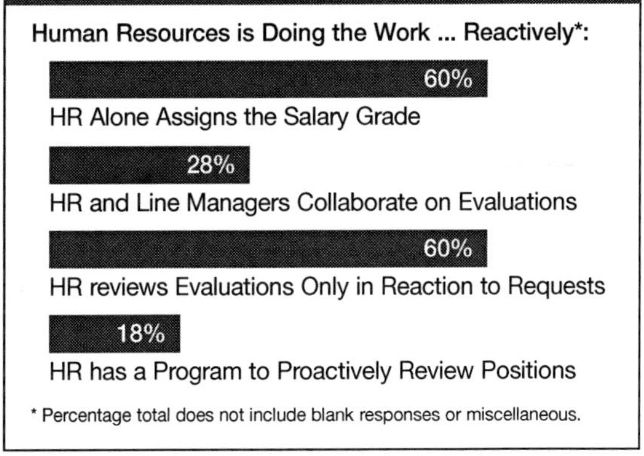

Human Resources is Doing the Work ... Reactively*:

60%
HR Alone Assigns the Salary Grade

28%
HR and Line Managers Collaborate on Evaluations

60%
HR reviews Evaluations Only in Reaction to Requests

18%
HR has a Program to Proactively Review Positions

* Percentage total does not include blank responses or miscellaneous.

the company is misallocating 2 percent of its payroll. This is a significant cost since this error is more than one-half of most merit increases awarded this year. Of course, if an incorrect grade assignment is to a higher grade, then the company is paying employees more than its stated policy or what the market demands. Likewise, if employees are placed improperly in a lower grade, then the company has the increased cost of replacing its employees who might pursue better-paying jobs elsewhere as a result of not earning what the work is worth. This is particularly dangerous because the employees who typically leave are the "best and brightest" and are more likely to find employment opportunities elsewhere.

Designing and administering systems that determine the value of work or the value of the employee doing the work is, perhaps, the compensation professional's primary accountability. The data collected from more than 1,200 respondents indicated that companies might be paying a substantial financial price for not investing the necessary organization resources into valuing work. First, only 58 percent of compensation professionals who responded to the survey believed that 60 percent or more of their positions could be matched to the market. This combined with the observation that positions that cannot be matched to external compensation surveys are quite often positions that are designed uniquely within the organization, as well as those that provide the organization with competitive advantage. What reason, other than competitive advantage and value creation, would cause companies to design jobs so differently from other organizations that they cannot be matched to the market? Therefore, it is quite likely that organizations who do not have adequate market-pricing information on these unique positions nor an adequate internal work-valuing system are incurring risks of either overpaying these positions or increased probability of losing these critical employees if they are paid below where they should be.

The Perceived Effectiveness of Pay Programs

Compensation professionals were asked to evaluate the perceived effectiveness of various attributes of their compensation programs. These results, which are shown in Figure 9 on page 111, reveal some interesting findings.

- More than half of compensation professionals responding to the survey believe their job analysis and documentation process, and job evaluation processes, are effective or very effective, at 59 percent and 64 percent, respectively.
- Market-pricing processes are deemed effective or highly effective by 84 percent of respondents.
- Individual performance appraisal is judged effective or very effective by 59 percent of responding compensation professionals.

Overall, compensation professionals judge their compensation programs to be effective or highly effective as they relate to managing internal equity (75 percent), managing external competitiveness (80 percent) and the ability to attract and retain talent (81 percent). However, they judge their program's ability to motivate employees less positively (38 percent). The effectiveness of communicating the pay program is rated effective or highly effective by only 27 percent of respondents. The relatively higher effectiveness ratings on internal equity and external competitiveness management may also be attributable to the fact that the compensation department largely controls these programs. The relatively low effectiveness rating on the motivational value may be due to the fact that line managers within the organization need to work with the HR function to create an impact here — and this is challenging work for the organization.

Another potential cause for the perceived weak linkage between pay and motivation may rest with the finding that 68 percent of compensation professionals gave pay increases of less than two times the average increase to their high performers as compared to the average performers. A higher percentage of "Most Admired" companies reported rewarding top performers at two times or more than the average increase. There are clearly significant opportunities for HR to improve the quality of compensation through effective program implementation.

Future Directions

The information collected from this study offers insights and opportunities for creating higher-impact pay systems. First, it's important to recognize that the attributes of pay policies and program

FIGURE 9: Effectivenesses of Pay Practices as Evaluation by Respondents

Job analysis and documentation processes
Do not use	17
Not effective	2
Marginally effective	21
Effective	51
Very effective	8

Job evaluation or grading method
Do not use	18
Not effective	1
Marginally effective	18
Effective	53
Very effective	11

Process for employees to appeal job grading or salary decisions
Do not use	48
Not effective	4
Marginally effective	20
Effective	26
Very effective	3

Salary ranges
Do not use	9
Not effective	2
Marginally effective	14
Effective	58
Very effective	18

Market-pricing processes
Do not use	3
Not effective	1
Marginally effective	12
Effective	62
Very effective	22

Merit pay (i.e., salary increases based on performance)
Do not use	6
Not effective	4
Marginally effective	32
Effective	49
Very effective	9

Individual performance appraisal
Do not use	2
Not effective	6
Marginally effective	33
Effective	50
Very effective	9

Alignment between organization and individual performance goals
Do not use	7
Not effective	11
Marginally effective	38
Effective	38
Very effective	7

design for professional and managerial employees have not changed substantially over time. There is a predominance of more traditional, time-tested compensation program designs than the literature and variety of compensation experts might lead one to believe. In fact, most organizations do the following:

- Use both job evaluation and market pricing to place a value on their jobs.
- Attempt to pay near the middle of the labor market.
- Have pay ranges between 30 to 70 percent of midpoint.
- Adjust salary ranges annually.
- Make HR the dominant role in evaluating positions and assigning pay ranges.
- Provide base salary increases based on individual performance.
- Provide minimal pay communications to employees.

Research findings indicate that while the design of pay systems may indeed be "time tested," there is considerable room for improving the implementation of new pay policies and programs and enhancing the effectiveness of existing pay systems. Determining what constitutes a successful pay practice is critical because of the cost and motivation implications of pay systems that are either not designed or implemented effectively. The impact of pay policies and programs on employee behavior and motivation is significant, and HR has a major role to play: First, by guaranteeing that scarce organizational financial resources are focused where they should be, and second, by making sure that the organization has the right alignment between the business strategy and pay programs. Finally, compensation professionals need to ensure that the pay programs are effectively administered and kept up-to-date.

This research has confirmed the linkage between pay policies and programs and organizational effectiveness. Consequently, compensation professionals need to help management understand how compensation decisions are going to affect company competitiveness. By clarifying how compensation impacts the organization and taking leadership on compensation issues, enterprising HR has a critical role in building a successful organization.

Authors

Dow Scott, Ph.D., is a professor of human resources at Loyola University Chicago and president of Performance Development International Inc. His practical approach to teaching, research and consulting focuses on helping business leaders create more productive organizations and committed employees. He has been published in more than 100 journals, books and conference proceedings and also received national recognition for team/productivity improvement and HR research from the Academy of Management and the Society of Human Resource Management (SHRM). Scott's research and consulting has focused on employee retention, creation of effective teams, performance-improvement strategies, pay and incentive systems, evaluation of HR programs and the development of high-performance organizations.

Thomas D. McMullen (tom_mcmullen@haygroup) is a senior consultant and Midwest rewards practice leader in the Chicago office of Hay Group. He has 20 years of combined human resources practitioner and consulting experience. His work focuses primarily on total reward and performance program design, including rewards strategy development, incentive plan design, employee pay and job evaluation.

Prior to joining Hay, McMullen was in senior compensation roles with Kentucky Fried Chicken Corp. and Humana Inc. He holds a BS degree in mathematics and a master's degree in business administration from the University of Louisville.

Richard S. Sperling, CCP (Richard_sperling@haygroup.com) is a senior consultant in the Chicago office of Hay Group. He works with clients to design and value jobs, build effective organization structures, and develop and implement total rewards systems.

Sperling has designed leading-edge approaches to analyzing, understanding, designing and valuing work in clients' increasingly complex and varied organizational settings. He is a recognized expert in work comparison and valuing.

Sperling serves as client relationship manager for several of Hay Group's large clients, serving as the focal point to integrate the full range of Hay's consulting services to those clients in ways that support that client's business results and strategy.

Marc Wallace (marc_Wallace@haygroup.com) is an experienced consultant in performance management and compensation. He has presented for several regional organizations as well as at the WorldatWork annual conference on multiple occasions and national conferences on variable pay. As a consultant at Hay Group, Wallace works with organizations to develop strong rewards and performance management systems. Wallace holds a master's degree in international management from Thunderbird and a bachelor's degree in economics from the University of Wisconsin at Madison.

Reprinted from *WorldatWork Journal* Fourth Quarter 2003.

New Ways to Manage Pay
Upgrading Base Pay, Pay Progression and Variable Pay Plans to Attract and Retain Talent
By N. Frederic Crandall, Ph.D.

Downsizing, outsourcing, offshoring, new technology and basic changes in work design have radically changed the nature and value of work performed in organizations today. As a result, millions of jobs have been lost. More importantly to total rewards professionals, these changes have introduced new employee-skill requirements: broader jobs with upgraded skills and a shift from "doing" work to "coordinating" and "problem solving." The combination of job eradication and changes in skill requirements has left many companies with completely altered job structures. However, these structures are a result of more fundamental shifts in business strategy. For example, many companies have moved from a manufacturing to a marketing focus, or from a product to a service orientation. Overall, changes in the nature and value of work today are directly tied to the evolution of business strategy, which is moving at a rapid pace.

In the past, when job scope and value changed, compensation programs typically reacted through pay-realignment mechanisms, such as the re-evaluation of individual jobs or the assignment of temporary premium pay for "hot" jobs. But the massive changes in job structures we face today are different and more fundamental. As we have moved into economy recovery and growth, many companies are experiencing a shift in strategic emphasis that translates into new job structures, and in turn *should* translate into new metrics for base pay, progression pay and variable pay.

To meet these challenges, total rewards professionals need to understand the external forces that are causing jobs and job structures to change. In turn, we must understand the drivers of change inside the organization — how jobs and job structures are adapting to these external forces. Finally, we need to identify the requisite pay-management tools to attract new talent and retain top performers.

To gain this understanding, this article starts with an overview of five basic trends causing change, then discusses the introduction of pay-program value drivers and new tools for pay management.

Five Basic Trends and Their Impact

Five basic trends are driving the need for new pay-management tools:

- Continual downsizing and reductions in staff over the past 10 years have resulted in expanded work roles crossing traditional occupational boundaries.
- During the same period, enterprise IT platforms have led to upgraded skills required in jobs throughout organizations.
- Outsourcing and offshoring initiatives have moved much work out of the organization, resulting in redefined work objectives for remaining jobs.
- Transformations from departmental structures to process-based structures have changed the focus in many organizations from functional work to process-based work.
- Process-based work, in turn, has led to team-based work that replaces individually paced work.

To be sure, not all of these trends have had the same impact on all organizations. However, collectively they all have driven the nature of work unmistakably and unambiguously from a one-dimensional repetitive focus to a multidimensional knowledge-based and problem-solving focus. Figure 1 summarizes these trends.

The overriding theme of these five trends is the movement from jobs that are done independently to jobs that are focused on coordinating with other associates, and from work that is routine to work that is focused on problem solving. Traditional ways of defining and valuing work, through job duties and responsibilities, provide neither an accurate picture of these changes nor a meaningful index of value.
A new way of defining work are needed to deliver value now and in the future. Value-driven metrics for pay programs also is needed to attract new talent and keep top performers. For example, new metrics are required to place value on solving unique problems and coordinating solutions that arise in the course of a normal day's work.

Following is an overview of the core elements of work that are emerging as value drivers and can be translated into new tools of pay management. They are focused on the skills and competencies required to deliver value today and in the future.

FIGURE 1: The Changing Nature of Work		
Trend:	From:	To:
Expanded Work Roles	Single-skilled job	Multiskilled job
Upgraded Skill Components of Work	Repetitive tasks	Problem-solving tasks
Outsourcing and Offshoring	"Doing" the work of the organization	"Coordinating" the work of the organization
Process-based Work	Functions operate as silos	Functions collaborate to manage process and projects
Team-based Work	Individuals complete work independently	Members of team share the work

Defining Skills and Competencies

There are three distinct types of competencies:

- Strategic Competencies: mission-critical skills that are required to achieve competitive advantage
- Process Competencies: reflect the knowledge and skills involved in the work itself
- Individual Competencies: the characteristics that underlie an individual's ability to be effective.

Strategic competencies define what sets us apart from the rest, process competencies describe what we do and individual competencies define who we are. Following is a brief overview of the three competency types.

Strategic Competencies

Mission-critical skills (MCS) contribute to competitive advantage and differentiate an organization from its competitors. They represent the foundation for creating value in an organization. For example, product innovation is critical for 3M Corp., consistency is critical for McDonald's and high-quality service is critical for Ritz-Carlton Hotels.

Process Competencies

Process competencies are derived from an organization's business processes that cross functional boundaries and represent how an organization delivers value to customers. The focus of process competencies is on the work itself. Work can be tangible and linear as in manufacturing processes, or nonlinear and nonroutine, as in technical, financial and service processes.

Individual Competencies

Individual competencies are the underlying characteristics of the people who deliver value to the organization. Examples include flexibility, conscientiousness, a detail-oriented nature, sound judgment and a high-achievement orientation.

The Emerging Role of MCS

MCS are emerging as the key factor in transforming work. MCS are important for two reasons: First, MCS capture functionality across occupational boundaries and redefine organizational objectives. Second, they are directly tied to the organization's strategy drivers. By cutting across occupations in the organization, MCS become a common bond, promoting effective teamwork, flexibility and communication. Figure 2 on page 117 demonstrates examples of MCS.

Because MCS span across traditional occupational boundaries, a competency that embodies "value creation," for example, may include engineering, marketing and financial staff. In effect, MCS make the organization unique and can propel it ahead of the competition. MCS may change when an organization's overall mission or strategy

FIGURE 2: Examples of MCS

Skill Area	Description
Productivity	Getting the best use of your current asset base
Value Creation	Creating customer loyalty; lengthening product life cycle; focusing on new markets
New Product/Service Development	Application of the organization's creative talents to new opportunities with new or existing customers

changes. For example, an implication of outsourcing may be a change in strategy for an organization, which results in a need to change MCS. It is critical for compensation management to translate MCS into pay-program value drivers, and then use these value drivers as pay-management tools.

Pay-Program Value Drivers

Compensation involves an exchange from an organization to an individual or group for work performed. Compensation is a "value driver" if the exchange maintains and strengthens the chain of value from the combination of capital and human assets that creates the value and ends with the ultimate customer. While compensation takes many forms, let us consider three components of direct compensation, which include the following:

- **Base Pay.** The competitive market-based hourly or weekly/monthly salary earned for performing a specific role.
- **Base Pay Progression.** Base pay movement over time for individual performance, competency development, skill acquisition and/or job growth.
- **Variable Pay.** Incentive or bonus pay that is paid in addition to fixed components. Earnings may be based on preset goals or paid at the discretion of the company for individuals, groups or the whole company.

Because value drivers are based on the three levels of competency, the value of each element of direct compensation also is based on a combination of these three competencies. Following is an overview of each element of direct compensation. These elements are summarized in Figure 3 on page 118.

Base Pay Value Drivers

Value is delivered through base pay by individual competencies, process competencies and MCS. Base pay value in most organizations is based primarily on the external competitive marketplace. The job market places a value on the individual competencies (e.g., tickets to the ballpark) as a foundation. Atop this foundation, process competencies represent the value of the experience and skill required to do the work. Finally, MCS represent the value of the capability to drive the organization's strategic objectives.

	Base Pay Value Driver	Base Pay Progression Value Driver	Variable Pay Value Driver
Competencies			
Individual Competencies	Value based on innate individual characteristics and behaviors (e.g., "tickets to the ballpark")	Must exhibit individual competencies to be eligible for full pay progression award	Must exhibit individual competencies to be eligible for full variable pay award
Process Competencies	Value based on process competencies (e.g., work activities) possessed and demonstrated	Value based on additional process competencies acquired and demonstrated	Must exhibit process competencies to be eligible for full variable pay award
Mission Critical Skills	Value based on MCS (e.g., skills related to business strategy) possessed and demonstrated	Value based on additional MCS acquired and demonstrated	Value based on achievement of goals driven by MCS

FIGURE 3: **Pay Program Value Drivers**

Progression Pay Value Drivers

Progression pay is allocated to individuals both as an annual base pay adjustment and as a promotion to a higher position in the organization. Progression pay is derived from each of the three competency sources: continuing to exhibit the innate personal characteristics embodied in individual competencies; acquisition and demonstration of additional process competencies; and the acquisition and demonstration of additional MCS.

Variable Pay Value Drivers

Value embodied in incentive or bonus pay also is derived from all three sources. Similar to pay progression, continuing to exhibit individual competencies is a foundation for the value attached to variable pay. Now add the demonstration of process competencies as a core expectation, as well. The lack of value is observable if these characteristics are not exhibited, which leads to the withholding of incentive bonuses. Positive value is derived from MCS through the achievement of strategic objectives and organizational goals.

Pay-Management Tools

The tools of pay management (competitive pay positioning, a pay-for-performance pay-adjustment matrix and positioning incentive targets at competitive pay levels) can be used to transform the value drivers that are summarized in Figure 4 on page 119 into a comprehensive direct pay program. Following is an overview of these tools.

Base Pay Tools

Competitive pay positioning at a premium level for MCS (e.g., 75th percentile) provides a means to attract and retain MCS-related jobs. (A thorough analysis of jobs

FIGURE 4: Pay-Management Tools

Competencies	Base Pay Tools	Progression Pay Tools	Variable Pay Tools
Individual Competencies	50th-percentile match on comparable skills from peer organizations with parallel individual competencies (presumes hiring-process screens for individual competencies)	Downward adjustment and/or ineligibility for not possessing and demonstrating individual competencies	Downward adjustment and/or ineligibility for not possessing and demonstrating individual competencies
Process Competencies	50th-percentile match on comparable skills from peer organizations with relevant process competencies	Pay adjustment based on acquisition and demonstration of process competencies	Downward adjustment and/or ineligibility for not possessing and demonstrating process competencies
Mission-Critical Skills	75th-percentile match on jobs that are MCS heavy	Pay adjustment premium for jobs that are MCS heavy; promotion premium for jobs that are MCS heavy	Incentive targets based on financial, operational and customer goals; incentive premium for jobs that are MCS heavy

and job families is required to correctly identify MCS-related jobs before assigning a premium. These jobs are not necessarily in high demand in the marketplace, but are nevertheless critical for the organization.)

Progression Pay Tools

If associates do not possess or demonstrate individual competencies, then progression pay adjustments should be downward adjusted or withheld. The pay adjustment matrix should have a premium for MCS-heavy jobs. Also, promotion policy should include a premium for MCS-heavy jobs.

Variable Pay Tools

Variable pay should be treated similarly to progression pay by downward adjusting or withholding pay if individual or process competencies are not possessed or demonstrated. For MCS-heavy jobs, there should be a premium for incentive targets.

Looking Ahead

As business strategy and operations undergo a generational shift, total rewards professionals need to change the tools of pay management to attract new talent and retain top performers. By linking pay to individual competencies, process competencies and mission-critical skills, a clear line of sight is established between mutual expectations and rewards.

Authors

N. Frederic Crandall, Ph.D., (fredc@cwelink.com) is the director of CWE/Crandall Ltd. His primary role involves assisting clients in executing strategy through effective organizations and compensation systems. Crandall was a faculty member of the Cox School of Business at Southern Methodist University. He holds an A.B. from the University of California at Berkeley; and M.S. in business administration from the Anderson School of Management at the University of California at Los Angeles; and a Ph.D. in industrial relations from the University of Minnesota.

Author's Note

Material for this article is drawn from Chapter 42, "New Tools for Pay Management," of *The Compensation Guide*, edited by William Caldwell and published by Thomson/West Inc. The chapter is written by N. Frederic Crandall and John M. Bremen of Watson Wyatt Worldwide. Material also is drawn from an earlier version of chapter 42 of *The Compensation Guide*, authored by N. Frederic Crandall, Marc J. Wallace Jr., John M. Bremen and Mary Schulze.

Reprinted from *WorldatWork Journal* Third Quarter 2004.

Compensation in the Hot Seat
By John M. Bremen

For the past 10 years, compensation professionals have worked to earn a "seat at the table." In practical terms, this has involved changing the role of compensation to one of strategic adviser and business partner to senior management, as opposed to that of administrator. Regular *workspan* readers may have noticed several articles on this topic in recent years.

The current dramatic changes in corporate governance standards, coupled with emerging tax, accounting and reporting regulations (not to mention a turbulent economic environment), have thrust routine aspects of the compensation function into the spotlight. Suddenly, compensation not only has a seat at the table, but that seat is hot.

Accordingly, compensation leaders across industries are asking themselves, "Now what?"

The good news is that compensation professionals — many of them already serving as trusted business advisers to management — have a greater opportunity to drive the bottom lines of their businesses in several ways. The bad news is, the level of change in the profession is somewhat overwhelming to many groups.

Why the Change?

Traditionally, businesspeople have viewed compensation as a cost center. In fact, for many businesses, compensation has represented the single largest set of costs. As a result, cost management has been the name of the game for the compensation function.

In the 1980s, businesses realized that compensation programs — when strategically designed — could actually encourage specific levels of employee performance and help drive both the top and bottom lines of the income statement. This realization not only shifted the priorities of many compensation professionals, it also made vice presidents of operations, sales, marketing and finance aware of compensation's potential benefits to the business.

In the 1990s, the rapid economic growth and subsequent "war for talent" put additional emphasis on compensation. Again, compensation professionals had —

and took — the opportunity to affect the business, this time by reducing turnover, helping increase the company's competencies and talent and using pay to drive growth.

Perhaps nothing could have prepared the profession, however, for what was to come following the turn of the millennium. Three simultaneous sets of factors transformed the focus on pay virtually overnight (see Figure 1).

Economic Turbulence

The economic downturn that began in the early 21st century put immediate pressure on compensation. Merit budgets shrank dramatically or disappeared altogether. Incentive plans missed payouts for the first time in recent memory. Issues such as underwater stock options and high overhang plagued long-term incentive plans.

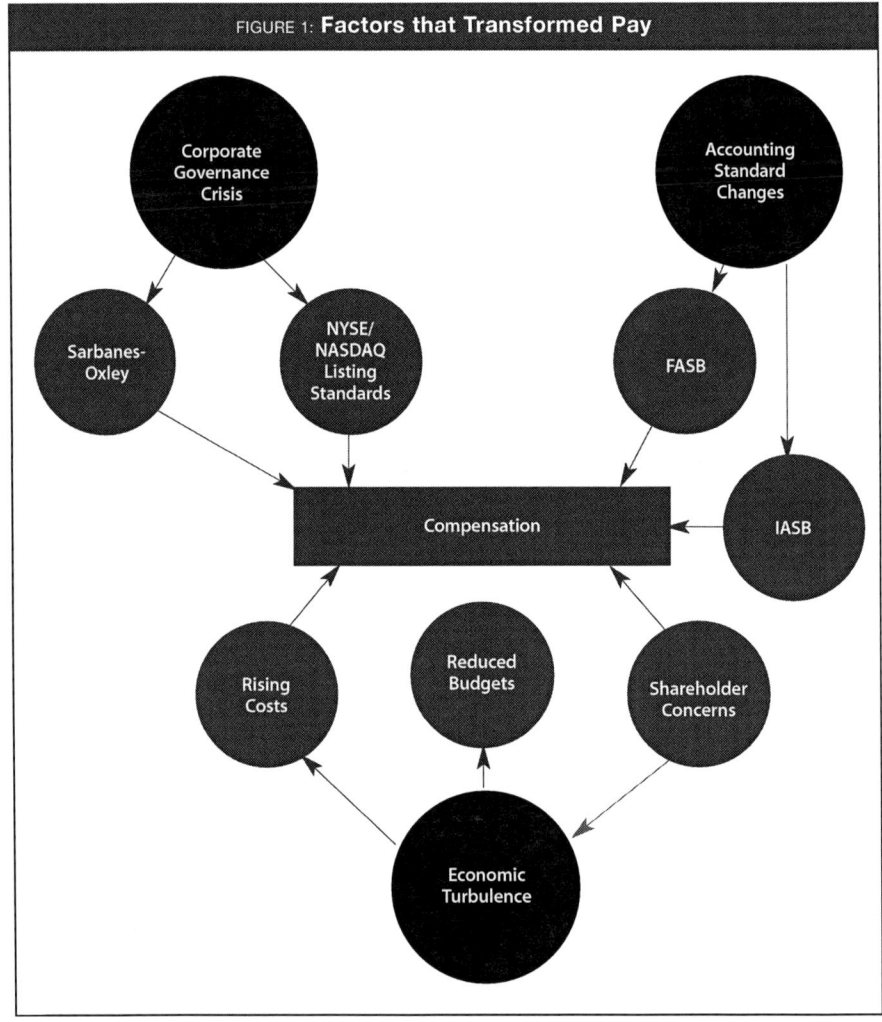

FIGURE 1: **Factors that Transformed Pay**

Surprisingly, however, many companies still found it difficult to attract and retain high performers and critical-skill employees. Suddenly, senior management was tapping compensation professionals on the shoulder to find ways of doing more with less, asking the tough business question, "How can we continue to drive performance with substantially fewer resources?" As it became apparent that the downturn would not be a short one, compensation professionals became involved with senior management for the long haul.

Corporate Governance Crisis

The ensuing corporate governance crisis, which led to the Sarbanes-Oxley Act and revised listing standards for the major stock exchanges, put compensation professionals into uncharted territory as governance and compliance issues had new and substantive impact on many existing plans and routine pay transactions.

Further, boards of directors deepened their focus on compensation matters, with compensation committees, audit committees, finance committees and governance committees initiating broad reviews of all aspects of pay, often down to the level of performance measures, funding formulas and individual payout amounts. Compensation professionals, who had long struggled to get into the executive conference room, now found themselves in the boardroom.

Accounting Standard Changes

Subsequent changes to accounting standards by the International Accounting Standards Board (IASB) and the Financial Accounting Standards Board (FASB) deepened the relationship between compensation professionals and the CFO. While compensation experts had long dealt with issues such as tax treatment, 162(m) and 280G regulations, the new rules created a new dimension in complexity for long-term incentive plans. Combined with new governance standards relating to performance-measure goal setting and calculation, the context surrounding incentive design was made even more complex.

As a result of these changes, it became common in any given month for senior compensation professionals to interact with the heads of human resources, sales, marketing, operations, accounting, audit, legal and compliance, as well as the CFO, CEO and board of directors. Suddenly, compensation was a long way from the back office.

Areas of Impact

Compensation's role has evolved from being focused on pure people issues to a more fundamental focus on business issues. As Figure 2 on page 124 illustrates, many traditional compensation responsibilities have been elevated in prominence to the strategic level. For example, a traditional focus on cost management has given way to treatment of compensation as a major investment. As such, companies are considering each compensation program as an investment vehicle — one is

FIGURE 2: Changing Compensation Responsibilities

Old World	New World
Cost management	Portfolio management (ROI)
Attraction and retention	Talent management (driving mission-critical skills and competitive advantage)
Motivation	Employee engagement and performance-management, (revenue growth, customer retention, operational productivity)
Compliance	Corporate governance and accountability (public opinion, shareholder opinion, risk management)

short-term, one is long-term, one focuses on value creation, another focuses on growth. In today's executive suite or boardroom, the discussion does not focus on program design, but rather on return on investment (ROI) and the bottom line.

What once was "attraction and retention" has given way to "talent management," or using compensation to drive the acquisition and development of mission-critical skills that enable a company to achieve a competitive advantage in its industry. What once was "motivation" is now "employee engagement and performance management." Coincidentally, in the February 2004 *Harvard Business Review*, balanced scorecard founders Robert Kaplan and David Norton identified direct links between human-capital management and company performance to factors such as revenue growth, customer retention and operational productivity — all areas that directly affect financial outcomes.

Finally, what once was "compliance" has given way to "corporate governance and accountability," aspects of which compensation professionals impact every day, ultimately leading to short- and long-term direction in public opinion, shareholder satisfaction and risk management.

Impact on Compensation's Role

"The role of the compensation professional has evolved to play a much more value-added role in the business," according to Dave Gustat, a WorldatWork Compensation Advisory Board member, who is director of compensation at Sears Roebuck & Co. As Figure 3 shows, this evolution involves many facts of the role, including a shift from internal to external focus, and from implementer to adviser.

FIGURE 3: The Evolution of Compensation's Role

Old World	New World
• Transactions	• Strategy
• Administration	• Design
• Conference room	• Board room
• Internally focused	• Externally focused
• Middle management	• C suite
• Enforcer	• Enabler
• HR skills	• HR skills *plus* finance and strategy
• Implementer	• Adviser

What to Do about It

"The most important thing compensation professionals can do is be holistic — acknowledging multiple constituencies with competing interests; courageous — advocating your best thinking may create conflict with powerful people; and independent — respectfully managing influences in order to maintain your professional integrity and ethics," said Mark Englizian, CCP, GRP, director of global compensation with Amazon.com and chairman of the WorldatWork Society of Certified Professionals.

Following are four distinct actions that compensation leaders and professionals can take to maximize their contributions "at the table" and maintain their position there as true business partners:

- **Be a "Business Person" First and a "Compensation Person" Second.** While compensation professionals cannot and should not ever violate or abandon the basic tenets of sound compensation design, they should focus on the broader business issues at hand. As such, consider beginning each management or board interaction with a discussion of key business issues at hand, then transition into specifics surrounding pay design or administration. The conclusion of any interaction should include a clear and specific statement regarding business impact (e.g., ROI, competitive advantage, revenue growth, customer satisfaction, productivity, shareholder opinion), as well as a mutual understanding of all relevant process issues, outcomes and next steps.

- **Develop Requisite Financial Skills.** In the past, it was possible for senior-level compensation experts to get by without deep financial or accounting skills. Increasingly, compensation leaders are expecting professionals to possess new skills. In fact, many leaders have shifted potential sources of talent from the HR generalist track to the finance track. While the long-term direction of this shift remains unclear, compensation and other HR professionals can significantly increase their career potential by growing requisite financial and accounting skills. According to WorldatWork Compensation Advisory Board Member Connie L. Haney, CCP, GRP, director of global compensation services at Cargill Inc., "If you can demonstrate both HR and financial skills, you've got a very powerful value proposition to your employer."

- **Develop a Clear Compensation Governance Process.** With all of the diverse stakeholders focused on compensation today, compensation groups are wise to develop a process that does the following:
  - Satisfies all regulatory, statutory and exchange governance standards
  - Aligns with the company's business strategy and culture
  - Meets the needs of the various executive stakeholders from a business perspective
  - Remains appealing to and engages the employee population

- Remains market competitive
- Does not drive you crazy.

Due to the complexity of related interactions, a poorly conceived process will be ineffective on many levels (e.g., governance design) and cause high levels of professional frustration and burnout.

- **Consider Longer-term Skill Requirements and Career Paths.** As the role of the compensation professional continues to evolve, so too will the skill requirements and career paths across the profession. As such, compensation leaders would be well served by planning for the future today. If financial skills are needed, start training now. If board-level presentation skills are required, acquire them before the next meeting. If sources of talent need to be adjusted, the process could take some forethought and several iterations.

(See "Key Questions to Consider in Relation to Your Company.")

SIDEBAR: **Key Questions to Consider in Relation to Your Company**

- Do compensation professionals have the business acumen and financial knowledge to be responsive to these new demands? If not, how can these competencies be gained?
- Is there a clear and ongoing partnership between compensation and finance? If not, is this a gap?
- Is the career path between HR and compensation becoming limited? If so, what should be done?
- What additional skills/knowledge do compensation professionals need to be effective in meetings with senior leaders/board members?

In short, members of the profession should embrace their newfound seat at the table — and be prepared to sit there for many years to come as an active, value-added business partner and contributor, which may require a change in their own mindsets, as well.

About the Author

John M. Bremen leads Watson Wyatt's compensation practice in Chicago. He has been a WorldatWork member since 1988 and is a member of the Compensation Advisory Board. He can be reached at john.bremen@watsonwyatt.com or 312/525-2208.

Author's Note

The author wishes to recognize the contributions of all members of the Compensation Advisory Board. Their input was a core element of and vital to the content of this article.

Reprinted from *workspan* August 2004.

The Future of Compensation Professionals: According to Your Colleagues

By Barbara Manny, Thomas D. McMullen and Richard S. Sperling, CCP, and Dow Scott, Ph.D.

As Bob Dylan sang, "The times they are a changing." With opportunities to be more involved in major business decisions, compensation professionals have been asked to solve more difficult problems and face more difficult challenges. In turn, the profession needs to be able to step out of the comfort zone and be ready to seize these opportunities. From a survey of compensation professionals, it has become clear they feel their roles in the organization's strategic business plans are growing. Only time will tell if compensation professionals' perceptions will become reality.

In May 2005, the authors conducted a survey to find out what compensation professionals think about the future of the profession. From the two groups of compensation and HR professionals who had compensation responsibility — Chicago Compensation Association (CCA) members and a sample of WorldatWork members — there were 200 survey respondents.

Looking Ahead

Surprisingly, 75 percent of survey respondents believe that their companies are going to add more resources in the compensation function. However, past experience has shown compensation professionals need to prove their value to the organization through increased efficiencies and use of technology. Even more, they need to be valued business partners to organizations' line executives.

In general, the survey indicated that compensation professionals feel they will have greater involvement *across the board* in terms of providing design, administration and control support to their organizations. They also predict they will be substantially more involved in the design and administration of *incentive programs* over the next three to five years (See Figure 1 on page 129.) Given the shift away from stock option grants to other types of incentive vehicles, this comes as no surprise.

Survey respondents also report they will be more involved in salary budget planning in the future. Given the global competitive pressures most businesses are experiencing in today's economic environment, focusing on the size and allocation of the organization's compensation budget has become a priority. Compensation is one of

FIGURE 1: Compensation Professionals-Five-Year Predictions

Predictions	Mean	Much Less (1)	Less (2)	No Change (3)	More (4)	Much More (5)
Responsible for designing incentive pay programs	3.98	1%	2%	19%	55%	23%
Involved in designing executive pay programs	3.94	0%	3%	25%	54%	18%
Responsible for developing the organization's compensation strategy	3.93	0%	2%	24%	55%	19%
Involved in designing international or global compensation	3.92	1%	3%	24%	47%	25%
Involved in managing international or global compensation	3.87	1%	5%	24%	48%	22%
Involved in legal issues	3.78	0%	4%	34%	46%	16%
Involved in developing compensation budgets	3.70	0%	2%	37%	51%	10%
Responsible for recognition plans	3.66	0%	5%	35%	51%	9%
Involved in market-pricing or pay surveys	3.63	1%	4%	42%	39%	14%
Responsible for performance management	3.62	2%	9%	35%	43%	11%
Responsible for career pathing or leveling	3.54	0%	6%	34%	52%	8%
Responsible for administering incentive pay programs	3.47	2%	12%	29%	48%	9%
Involved in work valuing or job evaluation	3.45	1%	10%	41%	41%	7%
Involved in establishing pay ranges	3.40	1%	4%	59%	29%	7%
Involved in using pay for skills or knowledge programs	3.37	1%	15%	37%	40%	7%
Involved in establishing pay grades	3.36	1%	6%	57%	30%	6%
Involved in job analysis	3.35	1%	12%	47%	32%	8%
Outsourced by companies (excluding employee benefits)	3.22	5%	17%	37%	37%	4%
Responsible for individual employees' pay decisions	2.94	7%	25%	36%	28%	4%

the largest expenditures for most organizations, and it often is the largest controllable expenditure. Compensation professionals are primary stewards in one of the key financial areas of the business, and they should embrace their role in order to add value to the bottom line.

Global and executive compensation also were high on the lists of predicted responsibilities that would require greater involvement of compensation professionals, along with the responsibility for the development of the organization's compensation strategy.

From the Boardroom

The highly publicized mishandling of executive pay has moved compensation philosophy and strategy into the spotlight and the boardroom. Compensation professionals have had to transition from being viewed as the "compensation cops," i.e., monitoring and controlling costs, to being seen as a major business partner and contributor to the organization's success (or failure).

Effective compensation professionals today must play multiple roles: financial analyst, psychologist, coach, trusted adviser and problem solver. To accomplish this, they must immerse themselves in the organization's business, understanding its strategy, products, services, markets, revenue streams, critical success factors and, of course, employees' impacts on the business, as well as their needs and wants.

The survey results support the perception that compensation professionals must take on more responsibility for many areas impacting organization effectiveness, including performance management, career pathing and leveling, recognition plans and legal issues. The context in which the compensation professional operates also is becoming more challenging. The survey signals substantial perceived changes occurring in the following areas — employment law, global pay practices, performance management, executive pay and short-term variable pay.

In addition, recent research conducted by Hay Group, Loyola University of Chicago and WorldatWork shows that compensation professionals typically think more time and emphasis will be spent in most compensation programs and processes — from design to communication. But how can this be true if the staffing levels within the compensation function are expected to hold constant or increase only slightly? Some plausible explanations are the following:

- The continued trend toward outsourcing
- More leveraging of technology to support the administrative side of compensation
- Sharing the accountability for the design, administration and control of the compensation program with line management and/or the financial function.

There is a tendency for compensation to partner with line management and finance in the management of a compensation program. As shown in Figure 2 on page 131,

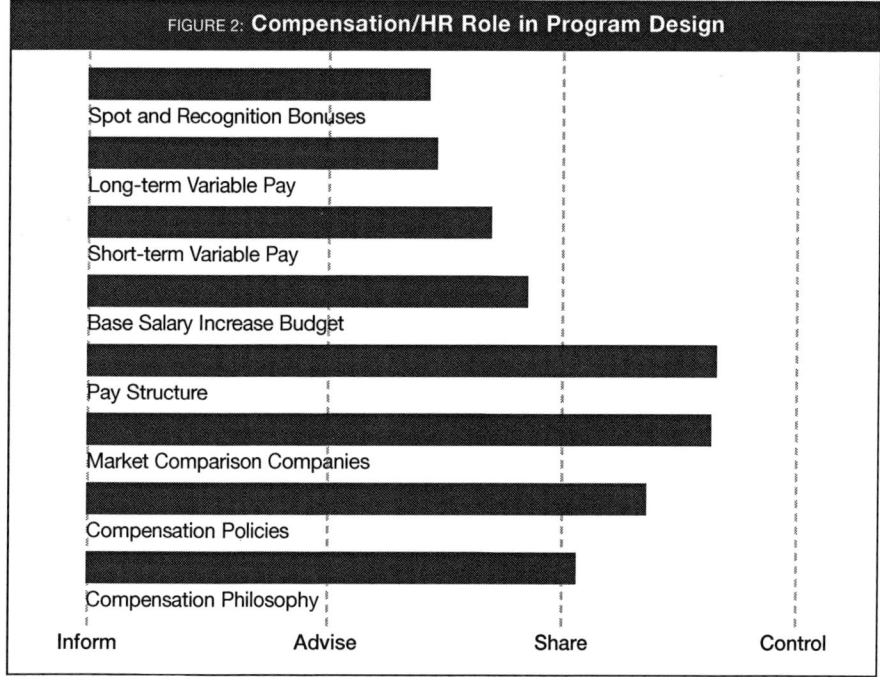

the compensation function tends to be more directly accountable for the design aspects of the compensation program, especially in the areas of compensation philosophy, policy development, market comparisons and development of pay structures. Line management and/or senior management tends to take a more active role in the design of spot and recognition programs and in the design of variable pay programs.

However, compensation tends to have more of an impact on compensation program *design* than on the *administration and control* of the compensation program. (See Figures 3 and 4 on page 132.) In addition, management and finance tend to take either shared or direct accountability for these dimensions of compensation program management. The administration or determination of base salary, variable pay or special compensation expenditures is typically an advisory to shared role of the compensation professional. And line managers have significant decision- making ability. Monitoring compensation expenditures, whether it's base salary, variable pay or recognition pay, is not predominately controlled by compensation, although the compensation professional typically would have an advisory role to management in the control of these expenditures.

It seems that the role of compensation professionals will continue to trend toward strategic organization counselors as opposed to administration and compliance officers, since the time just will not be available. While the fiscal control of compensation programs still remains a key strategic objective for compensation

FIGURE 3: **Compensation/HR Role in Program Administration**

FIGURE 4: **Compensation/HR Role in Program Monitoring and Control**

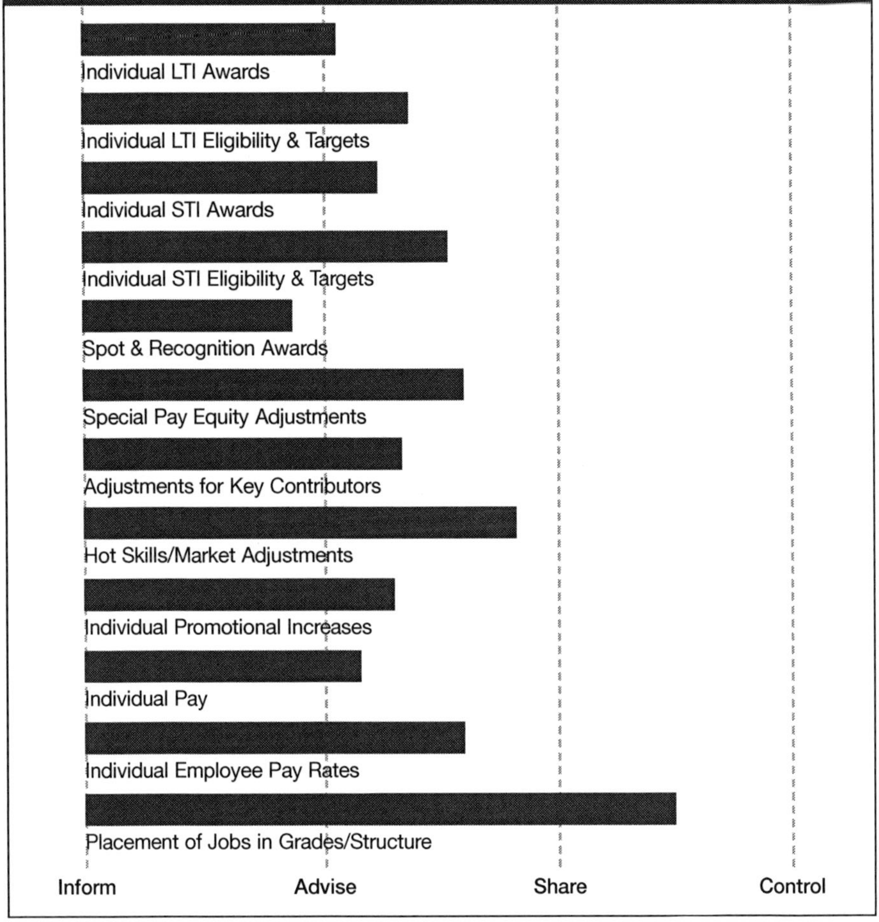

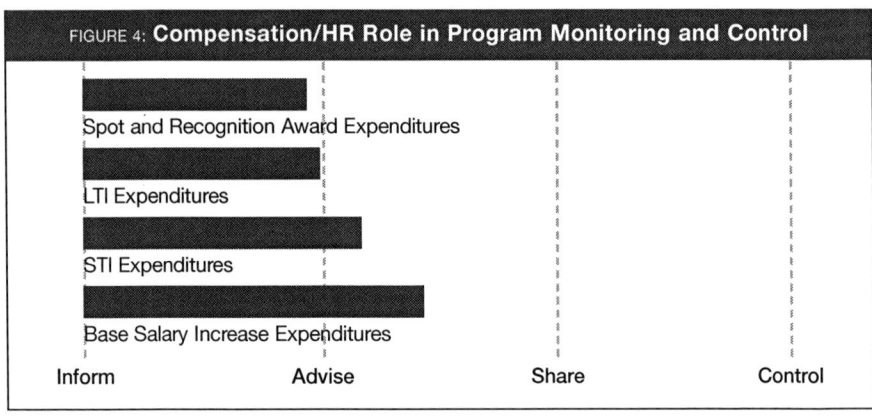

professionals, the real key will be the methods used to effectively leverage technology and outsourcing to make this viable.

The top five competencies identified by the 2005 WorldatWork survey for compensation professionals were:
- Strategic thinking
- Understanding company operations
- Project management
- Developing the business case for change
- Executive-level presentation skills.

What Will the Future Hold?

Survey respondents believe that the role of the compensation professional will be more challenging and demanding, and indeed, much more interesting. As such, compensation professionals must maintain and enhance the body of knowledge and find new ways to add value. With this more strategic role, compensation professionals should be prepared to take responsibility for business success. Survey respondents are positive about the opportunities for compensation. Only time will tell if they have accurately predicted the future.

About the Authors

Barbara Manny is the president of Benefits & Compensation Resources (BCR), a compensation and benefits consulting firm. She can be reached at b-cresources@msn.com or 847/236-1208.

Richard S. Sperling, CCP, is a senior consultant in the Chicago office of Hay Group. He can be reached at richard_sperling@haygroup.com or 312/228-1837.

Thomas D. McMullen is a senior consultant and Midwest Reward practice leader in the Chicago office of Hay Management Consultants. He can be reached at tom_mcmullen@haygroup.com or 312/228-1848.

Dow Scott, Ph.D., is a professor of human resources in the School of Business Administration at Loyola University Chicago and president of Performance Development International Inc. He can be reached at dscott@luc.edu or 312/915-6597.

Reprinted from *workspan* January 2006.

Glossary

A

across-the-board increase
An identical pay raise — either in a flat rate such as cents per hour or as a percentage of salary — given to all eligible employees. Also known as a general increase.

aging survey data
The practice of increasing market-survey data by an assumed percentage representative of wage movement to bring the data to a consistent point in time. This practice also is known as "advancing" or "trending" the data.

Americans with Disabilities Act of 1990 (ADA)
A federal law that creates nondiscrimination protections for people with disabilities, similar to Title VII of the Civil Rights Act of 1964, which is extended to other minorities. Under the law, employers may not refuse to hire or promote a person because of a disability, and employers are required to make "reasonable accommodations" to allow people with disabilities to perform essential functions. Regulations are enforced by the Equal Employment Opportunity Commission (EEOC).

anniversary date
1) The date used by insurance companies for the purpose of determining the experience rating for the completed accounting period and establishing the premium rates for the next period. (2) The date used in some pay systems to trigger a review of the employee's salary and/or to trigger a potential salary increase. It may be the anniversary of hiring, last pay increase, promotion or some other reference point.

annual bonus
Usually a lump-sum payment (cash, shares, etc.) made once a year in addition to an employee's normal salary or wage for a fiscal or calendar year. Generally nondiscretionary and not based on predetermined performance criteria or standards.

annualized increase percent
A salary increase expressed as an annual rate of increase. It is calculated by dividing the number of months since the last increase (denominator) into 12 (numerator) and multiplying the result by the actual percent increase: (12/number of months since last increase) x (percent increase).

average frequency (of salary increases)
Used to determine how often a salary increase is granted. It is determined by summing the months between increases granted for the employee groups and dividing by the number of increases and employees. Normally calculated on a departmentwide or companywide basis.

average hourly earnings
Used to determine the amount an employee has earned over a period of time. It is determined by dividing hours worked per period into the total wages earned for that period.

average percent increase
Used to determine the average salary increase given. It is calculated by dividing the sum of salary increase amounts for all eligible employees by the eligible payroll. Both the numerator and the denominator include those who were eligible and participated but received no increase.

B

base pay
The fixed compensation paid to an employee for performing specific job responsibilities. It is typically paid as a salary, hourly or piece rate.

base pay structure
The hierarchy of job grades and pay ranges established within an organization. The salary structure may be expressed in terms of job grades, job-evaluation points or policy lines.

benchmark job
A job that is commonly found and defined, and used to make pay comparisons, either within the organization or to comparable jobs outside the organization. Pay data for these jobs are readily available in published surveys.

benefits
Programs that an employer uses to supplement the cash compensation an employee receives. Benefits include publicly mandated and voluntary private "income protection" programs that often are provided through insurance, pay for time not worked and other employee perquisites.

broadbanding
A pay structure that consolidates a large number of pay grades and salary ranges into much fewer broadbands with relatively wide salary ranges, typically with 100 percent or more difference between minimum and maximum.

Bureau of Labor Statistics (BLS)
The principle fact-finding agency for the federal government in the broad field of labor economics statistics. Useful statistics include: CPI, NCS data, labor statistics, and other wage and benefits data.

C

cash compensation
The sum of all cash payments made to an individual for services (i.e., employment) during a given year.

central tendency
In statistics, some clustering around a central value in a distribution of data usually determined by one of the measures of location; i.e., mean, median or mode.

classification method of job evaluation
A nonqualitative form of job content evaluation that compares jobs to predefined class descriptions established for each job grade. Jobs are placed in whichever classification best describes them.

COLA
See cost-of-living adjustment.

collective bargaining agreements
Agreements between employee groups and employers detailing work conditions including working hours, vacation and holiday entitlements, termination-of-service provisions and sometimes benefit entitlements. These agreements may be specific to one company or industry or apply nationally.

common review date
The date on which all (or a group of) employees receive pay increases. For example, a company may implement increases for all employees on April 1; employees hired off cycle usually receive prorated increases. Also known as focal point review date.

comparable worth
The doctrine that men and women who perform work of the same "inherent value" should receive similar levels of compensation. According to this doctrine, jobs have an inherent value that can be compared across jobs of quite different content. Those accepting this position maintain that women performing jobs of comparable worth to those performed by men should be paid the same as men, excepting allowable differences (for example, seniority plans, merit plans, production-based pay plans or different locations).

compa-ratio
The ratio of an actual pay rate (numerator) to the midpoint or some other control point for the pay range (denominator). Compa-ratios are used to measure and monitor an individual's actual rate of pay to the midpoint or control point of his or her range. A compa-ratio can be calculated for a group, a department or an entire organization.

compensable factor
Any factor used to provide a basis for judging job value to create a job worth hierarchy (job evaluation). The generic compensable factors established by the Equal Pay Act of 1963 are skill, effort, responsibility and working conditions.

compensation
Cash provided by an employer to an employee for services rendered. Compensation comprises the elements of pay (e.g., base pay, variable pay, stock, etc.) that an employer offers an employee in return for his or her services.

compensation cost
The total cost to the organization, including the unrealized or unknown future cost effects of today's compensation decisions regarding the total compensation program. Included are base pay, incentive opportunities, benefits costs and liabilities, perquisite costs, time-off programs (vacations, sick pay, etc.).

compensation philosophy
Ensures that a compensation program supports an organization's culture.

compensation policy
Ensures that a compensation program carries out the compensation strategy while supporting the compensation philosophy.

compensation strategy
The principles that guide design, implementation and administration of a compensation program at an organization. The strategy ensures that a compensation program, consisting of both pay and benefits, supports an organization's mission, goals and business objectives. It may also specify what programs will be used and how they will be administered.

competency
A behavior, attribute or skill that is a predictor of personal success.

competitive pay policy
The strategic decision an organization makes about which labor markets to use as comparison groups and how to set pay levels with respect to those groups. After choosing the comparison group, the organization must decide its market position with respect to the group.

compression
Pay differentials too small to be considered equitable. The term may apply to differences between 1) the pay of supervisors and subordinates, 2) the pay of experienced and newly hired personnel of the same job and 3) pay-range midpoints in successive job grades or related grades across pay structures.

control point
The point within a salary range representing the desired pay for a fully qualified, satisfactory performer in a job or group of jobs at a given time (usually the midpoint of the salary range).

corporate culture
The norms, beliefs and assumptions adopted by an organization to enable it to adapt to its external environment and internally integrate people and units. It is strongly influenced by the values and behavior of an organization's management. In turn, corporate culture influences both the behavior of the members of the organization and the quality of the work experience.

cost-of-living adjustment (COLA)
An across-the-board wage and salary increase or supplemental payment designed to bring pay in line with increases in the cost of living to maintain real purchasing power.

cost-of-living index
See Consumer Price Index.

D

Department of Labor (DOL)
A regulatory agency that administers and enforces several federal laws including the Equal Pay Act of 1963, Fair Labor Standards Act of 1938 (FLSA), Employee Retirement Income Security Act of 1974 (ERISA) and Family and Medical Leave Act of 1993 (FMLA). Agencies under the DOL include the Bureau of Labor Statistics (BLS), Employment Standards Administration and the Pension and Welfare Benefits Administration (PWBA).

direct observation
A job analysis technique that involves the direct observation of employee(s) actually performing work in order to understand job content. The method is typically used for highly repetitive production jobs.

disclaimer statement
A provision in a job description that states that job descriptions typically do not specify every duty or responsibility that an employee may be asked to perform; e.g., "May perform other duties as required."

E

earnings
Total wages or cash received during a specified period of time (e.g., pay period, month, year) for time worked or service rendered, including all regular pay, overtime, premium pay, bonuses, etc.

effective date
(1) The date on which a benefits plan or insurance policy goes into effect, and from which time coverage is provided. (2) The date on which increases in salary or pay rate go into effect.

Equal Pay Act of 1963
An amendment to the Fair Labor Standards Act of 1938 (FLSA) that prohibits gender-related pay differentials on jobs that are substantially equal in terms of skill, effort, responsibility and working conditions, and that are performed in the same location.

equity
Anything of value earned through the provision or investment of something of value. (1) In the case of compensation, an employee earns equity interest through the provision of labor on a job. Equity often is used as a fairness criterion (i.e., "equal treatment") in compensation. (2) On an organization's balance sheet, equity represents the book value of the owners' stake in the firm. See also shareholders' equity.

exempt employees
Employees who are exempt from the Fair Labor Standards Act of 1938 (FLSA) minimum wage and overtime provisions due to the type of duties performed. Include executives, administrative employees, professional employees and those engaged in outside sales as defined by the FLSA.

external equity
A measure of an organization's pay levels or bands or "going market rates" compared to those of its competitors. As a fairness criterion, external equity implies that the employer pays wages that correspond to prevailing, external market rates, as determined by market pricing.

F

Fair Labor Standards Act of 1938 (FLSA)
A federal law governing minimum wage, overtime pay, child labor and record-keeping requirements.

feedback
Information about the state or outcome of a system that can be used to modify or correct a system's operation. As the term usually is used with respect to compensation, it relates to the process in which supervisors give employees information about the status of their performance. Performance appraisals are an example of a feedback mechanism.

G

general increase
See across-the-board increase.

geographic differentials
Pay differences established for the same job based on variations in costs of living or costs of labor among two or more geographical areas.

green circle rate
A rate paid to an employee that is below the established pay range minimum for a specific job.

H

hourly
The rate of pay per hour for a job being performed. An "hourly" worker may be assigned to various rated jobs during any pay period and is paid the "rate" applicable to each job while working on it. The term hourly also is used to distinguish between nonexempt and exempt employees.

I

incumbent
A person occupying and performing a job.

internal equity
A fairness criterion that directs an employer to establish wage rates that correspond to each job's relative value to the organization.

J

job
The total collection of tasks, duties and responsibilities assigned to one or more individuals whose work has the same nature and level.

job analysis
The systematic, formal study of the duties and responsibilities that constitute job content. The process seeks to obtain important and relevant information about the nature and level of the work performed and the specifications required for an incumbent to perform the job at a competent level.

job component method of job evaluation
A quantitative form of job content evaluation that uses multiple regression of market-pay levels versus two or more independent variables to establish a job worth hierarchy.

job content evaluation method(s)
Methods that use job content as the primary determinant in developing a job worth hierarchy. With these methods, market-pay levels typically are a secondary influence on the job worth hierarchy. Point factor is the most commonly used method.

job description
A summary of the most important features of a job, including the general nature of the work performed (duties and responsibilities) and level (e.g., skill, effort, responsibility and working conditions) of the work performed. It typically includes job specifications that detail employee characteristics required for competent performance of the job. A job description should describe and focus on the job itself and not on any specific individual who might fill the job.

job documentation
Written information about job content typically resulting from job analysis efforts. Documentation includes, but is not limited to, job descriptions, completed questionnaires, interview notes and efficiency study reports.

job evaluation
A formal process used to create a job worth hierarchy within an organization. The two basic approaches are market data and the job content.

job specifications
A description of the worker characteristics (i.e., knowledge, skills, abilities and behaviors) required to competently perform a given job. These characteristics must be bona fide occupational qualifications (BFOQs). Specifications, which commonly are referred to as "hiring" or "background" requirements, should be written before advertising or interviewing candidates for an open position. They should support the essential functions identified during job analysis to reduce potential liabilities under the Americans with Disabilities Act (ADA).

job title
The descriptive name for the total collection of tasks, duties and responsibilities assigned to one or more individuals whose positions have the same nature of work performed at the same level. Job titles should describe the nature and level of work performed. Titles often include the organizational function (e.g., corporate remuneration analyst) or geographic responsibility (e.g., Eastern region sales manager).

job worth hierarchy
The perceived internal value of jobs in relationship to each other within an organization. The job worth hierarchy forms the basis for grouping similar jobs together and establishing salary ranges.

L

lag structure policy
This strategy dictates that the company will consciously set its pay equal to current market levels at the beginning of the year. The company will be "lagging" the market until the increase is implemented at the end of the year.

lead structure policy
The company has decided to "outpace" the market. Pay is not set at current market levels, but at anticipated market levels.

lead-lag structure policy
A salary practice that is halfway between a lag and a lead policy. An organization's structure is set at the beginning of the plan year to its anticipation of the level the competition will reach by the middle of the plan year. It leads the market during the first six months, matches the competitive pay at the middle of the year and lags the market during the past six months.

lump-sum increase
Any increase in pay that is made in the form of a single cash payment. The most common form is the lump-sum merit increase.

M

market adjustment
The percentage increase to organization, group or individual pay that is necessary to adjust it to the estimated market level.

market pricing
Relative to compensation, the technique of creating a job worth hierarchy based on the "going rate" for benchmark jobs in the labor market(s) relevant to the organization. Under this method, job content is considered secondarily to ensure internal equity after a preliminary hierarchy is established based on market-pay levels for benchmark jobs. All other jobs are "slotted" into the hierarchy based on whole-job comparison.

mean
A simple arithmetic average obtained by adding a set of numbers and then dividing the sum by the number of items in the set.

median
The middle item in a set of ranked data points containing an odd number of items. When an even number of items are ranked, the average of the two middle items is the median.

merit increase
An adjustment to an individual's base pay rate based on performance or some other individual measure.

midpoint
The salary that represents the middle of a given salary range or pay grade.

midpoint differential
The difference in wage rates paid in the midpoints of two adjacent grades. A midpoint progression is calculated by taking the difference between two adjacent midpoints as a percentage of the lower of the midpoints. Also known as the midpoint differential.

midpoint progression
See midpoint differential.

midpoint-to-midpoint differential
See midpoint differential.

mode
The category or value that occurs most frequently in a set of observations. In a frequency distribution, it is the category with the highest frequency. Sometimes there is more than one mode.

N

nature of work
Critical data about a job that reflect the job's duties and responsibilities.

nonexempt employees
Employees who are not exempt from the minimum wage and overtime pay provisions of the Fair Labor Standards Act of 1938 (FLSA).

nonquantitative job evaluation
A method that creates a job worth hierarchy based on the perceived value of the "whole job(s)" but does not employ quantitative methods (i.e., assigning evaluation "points"). Examples of nonquantitative methods are classification and ranking.

O

O*NET
O*NET OnLine is an application that was created for the general public to provide broad access to the O*NET database of occupational information. The O*NET database includes information on skills, abilities, knowledges, work activities and interests associated with occupations. This information can be used to facilitate career exploration, vocational counseling and a variety of human resources functions, such as developing job orders and position descriptions, and aligning training with current workplace needs.

occupation
A generalized job or family of jobs common to multiple organizations or industries.

organizational culture
See corporate culture.

overtime
Under the Fair Labor Standards Act of 1938 (FLSA), nonexempt employees must be paid one-and-a-half times their normal wage rates for all hours worked in excess of 40 in any workweek. Some states require overtime be calculated by other than a 40-hour week or at greater than $1\frac{1}{2}$ times normal wage rate.

P

pay for performance
Links pay (base and/or variable), in whole or in part, to individual, group and/or organizational performance.

pay grade
The grade to which a given type of job is assigned.

pay policy line
The level at which the organization decides to set its pay against the external market. Usually the midpoint of the salary structure is set as an estimate of the market going rate.

pay range
The range of pay rates, from minimum to maximum, established for a pay grade or class. Typically used to set individual employee pay rates.

pay-range overlap
The degree to which the pay ranges assigned to adjacent grades in a structure overlap. Numerically, the percentage of overlap between two adjacent pay ranges.

pay-range width
The width or spread of a pay range, measured by the ratio: width = (maximum pay − minimum pay)/minimum pay.

pay-trend line
A line fitted to a scatter plot that treats pay as a function of job values. The most common technique for fitting a pay-trend line is regression analysis.

percentile
A measure of location in a distribution of numbers that defines the value below which a given percentage of the data fall. For example, the 90th percentile is the point below which 90 percent of the data fall.

point-factor method of job evaluation
A quantitative form of job content evaluation that uses defined factors and degree levels within each factor (usually five to seven levels, which are also defined). Each factor is weighted according to its importance (to the organization). Job content descriptions are compared to definitions of the degree levels, and the corresponding points assigned to the appropriate level are then awarded to the job and added for all factors to determine the total job score. The total scores are used to create a job worth hierarchy.

position
The total duties and responsibilities requiring the employment of a single employee. The total number of positions in an organization equals the number of employees plus vacancies.

Q

quantitative job evaluation
A method that creates a job worth hierarchy by analyzing jobs in terms of specific factors and numerical indices. Examples of quantitative methods are job component and point factor.

R

range
(1) For a set of data, the difference between the maximum value and the minimum value.
(2) For a pay grade, the percentage by which the maximum pay exceeds the minimum.

range penetration
The level of an individual's pay compared to the total pay range (rather than compared with midpoint, as in compa-ratio). Range penetration is calculated as:
RP = (Pay − Range Minimum)/(Range Maximum − Range Minimum).

range spread
See pay-range width.

ranking method of job evaluation
The simplest form of job evaluation. A whole-job, job-to-job comparison, resulting in an ordering of jobs into a job worth hierarchy from highest to lowest.

rate
See wage rate.

reclassification
The (re)assignment of a job to a higher or lower grade or range in the organization's job worth hierarchy due to a job content (re)evaluation and/or significant change in the going rate for comparable jobs in the external labor market.

red circle rate
An individual pay rate that is above the established range maximum assigned to the job grade. The employee is usually not eligible for further base pay increases until the range maximum surpasses the individual pay rate.

S

salary
Compensation paid by the week, month or year (rather than per hour). Generally applies to jobs that are exempt from the provisions of the Fair Labor Standards Act of 1938 (FLSA), but in some cases, nonexempt jobs can be salaried as well.

salary grade
A group of jobs of the same or similar value, used for compensation purposes. All jobs in a salary grade have the same salary range: minimum, midpoint and maximum.

salary increase cost
(1) The cost of the increase in the current (i.e., first) year is determined by multiplying the eligible payroll by the average-increase percent and the participant rate, adjusted for the percent of the year the increase is in effect. (2) The annualized cost of the increase (future-year cost) is determined by multiplying the eligible payroll by the average-increase percent and the participant rate.

salary structure
The hierarchy of job grades and pay ranges established within an organization. The salary structure may be expressed in terms of job grades, job-evaluation points or policy lines.

scope
A set of quantifiable job characteristics that ascribe value to a job. Typical measures include sales volume, asset size of the organization, number of subordinates and size of budget managed.

secondary source of job information
See scope.

seniority
Status determined by the length of time an employee has worked for a given employer, often as the basis for rights, privileges and benefits. The term also may be used to reflect time worked for a division, group or specific occupation. Union contracts often provide for multiple seniority calculations.

Sherman Anti-Trust Act (1890)
A federal law passed to protect the public from abuses of corporate monopolies. However, in 1908, the Supreme Court ruled that it applied to unions, as well. In terms of compensation, the exchange of wage information can be seen as "price fixing" wages.

shift differential
Extra pay allowance made to employees who work on a shift other than a regular day shift (e.g., 9 a.m. to 5 p.m., Monday through Friday) if the shift is thought to represent a hardship, or if competitive organizations provide a similar premium. Shift differentials usually are expressed as a percentage or in cents per hour.

skill-based pay
A person-based compensation system based on the repertoire of skills an employee can perform, rather than the specific skill that the employee may be doing at a particular time. Pay increases generally are associated with the addition and/or improvement of the skills of an individual employee, as opposed to better performance or seniority within the system. The pay level generally is not dependent on whether any of the skills are utilized.

skills inventory
A planning tool that specifies all people currently employed by the organization and classifies them according to their skills, job assignments, age, gender and other factors relevant to human resources planning. The device is employed primarily as a way of classifying internal labor supplies for human resources planning.

slotting
The act of placing a job into a job worth hierarchy established by some other job-evaluation method. The method involves comparing the job to one or more jobs in an already established hierarchy. Consequently, it cannot be used as a stand-alone method.

step rates
Standard progression pay rates that are established within a pay range. Step rates usually are a function of time in grade and often are referred to as automatic. However, they also can be variable or can be used in conjunction with merit programs.

survey
The gathering of information about a situation. Often, surveys consist of sampling data from a population. Examples include a benchmark salary survey that collects pay data for benchmark jobs from a defined labor market; a maturity salary survey that collects both pay and experience data from a defined labor market for benchmark jobs or jobs in a given discipline at a given degree level; and a benefits survey that collects benefits data from a defined labor market.

T

target compa-ratio
The organization's planned average salary for the organization, group or individual divided by the corresponding average (or total) midpoint. Can also be calculated on total salaries and total midpoints.

total rewards
The monetary and nonmonetary returns provided to employees in exchange for their time, talents, efforts and results. Total rewards involve the deliberate integration of five key elements that effectively attract, motivate and retain the talent required to achieve desired business results.

V

variable pay
Compensation that is contingent on discretion, performance or results achieved. It may be referred to as pay at risk.

Selected References

Selected References
Articles

Astron Solutions. 2001. How Can I Create Employee Ownership Without Using Stock Options? Part II. October 15 Issue.

Compensation Consulting Consortium LLC. 2002. Effective Market-based Pay Systems.

Conference Board. 2002. Canadian Variable Pay Offers a Bonus for Unionized Workplaces. *Newsline.**

Crowe, Barbara; Siscovick, Ilene; Marjorie Pieper. 2003. Designing a Work Force Architecture for Merger Success. *WorldatWork Journal*, Third Quarter, 39-46.

Ellis, Christian M.; Halliburton, Amy J. 2002. Looking into the Crystal Ball of Base Pay. *WorldatWork Journal*, Fourth Quarter, 14-20.

Foote, David. 2001. The Whirling World of IT Pay. *workspan*, October, 30-35.

Gherson, Diane J. 2000. Getting the Pay Thing Right. *workspan*, June, 47-51.

Handel, Jeremy. 2002. Does It Matter What Employees Know About Pay? A Recent Study Says Yes. *Canadian News*. Second Quarter, 15-17.

Heneman, Robert L.; Mulvey, Paul W.; LeBlanc, Peter V. 2002. Improve Base Pay ROI by Increasing Employee Knowledge — *WorldatWork Journal*, Fourth Quarter, 21-27.

Heneman, Robert L. 2001. Work Evaluation: Current State of the Art and Future Prospects. *WorldatWork Journal*, Third Quarter, 65-70.

Hewitt Associates. 2004. Companies Revamping Executive Long-term Incentive Programs. *Newsline.**

Hill, Brad; Tande, Christine. 2006. New Rules: Paying for Performance. *workspan*, May, 44-46.

Ibanez-Frocham, Martin. 2002. Executive Pay the Latin Way: The Evolution in Compensation. *workspan*, May, 34-41.

Jantz, Amy. 2005. Total Compensation Mix. WorldatWork White Paper.

Manas, Todd. 2000. Combining Reward Elements to Create the Right Team Chemistry. *workspan*, November/December, 46-52.

Mercer Human Resource Consulting. 2006. Global Report Confirms Executive Pay Gap. *Newsline.**

Mercer Human Resource Consulting. 2005. U.S. Compensation Planning 2006: Caution Gives Way to Optimism. *Perspective Newsletter*, October.

Mercer Human Resource Consulting. 2003. Globalization Prompting Multinationals to Change Pay, Benefits Strategies. *Newsline.**

Mercer Human Resource Consulting. 2000. Shaping Performance with Base Pay.

Morris, Elizabeth. 2005. Job Component Method. WorldatWork White Paper.

Perspectives, 2005. Wage Bias — DOL Tackles Compensation Discrimination. *workspan*, March, 12-18.

Satterfield, Terry. 2000. Pay the Job or the Person, But Why Not Both? *workspan*, November/December, 6-8.

SMCL/Mercer. 2005. Salaries and Bonuses Generally Higher in Continental Europe than in the UK. *Newsline.**

Sung, Amy; Todd, Emory. 2004. Line of Sight: Moving Beyond the Catchphrase. *workspan*, October, 65-69.

Wanderer, Mike. 2000. Dot-comp — A 'Traditional' Pay Plan with a Cutting Edge. *WorldatWork Journal*, Fourth Quarter, 15-24.

Weeks, Sandra. 2002. Job Evaluation Is Alive and Well ... at Least in Canada. *WorldatWork Journal*, Fourth Quarter, 10-13.

Wright, Al. 2004. Making the Case for Automation. *workspan*, July, 50-54.

Zingheim, Patricia K.; Schuster, Jay R. 2003. Getting Back to Basics. *workspan*, May, 54-58.

**Available to WorldatWork members only*

Live Chat Transcripts (www.worldatwork.org/library)

Base Pay Solutions — Chat Transcript
Guest Speaker: Peter V. LeBlanc

Total Rewards Strategies — Chat Transcript
Guest Speaker: Steve Gross.

WorldatWork Research & Surveys (www.worldatwork.org/library/research/surveys)

Changing Role of Compensation — 2005

Fiscal Management of Compensation Programs — 2005

Survey of Compensation Policies and Practices — 2003

WorldatWork Bookstore (www.worldatwork.org/bookstore)

Clampitt, William H. 2005. *Employee Compensation Basics*. Scottsdale: WorldatWork.

Evans, Elaine M. 2006. *Compensation Basics for HR Generalists*. Scottsdale: WorldatWork.

Henderson, Richard I. 2003. *Compensation Management In A Knowledge Based World*. Upper Saddle River: Prentice Hall.

Martocchio, Joseph J. 2004. *Strategic Compensation: A Human Resource Management Approach — Third Edition*. Upper Saddle River: Prentice Hall.

Milkovich, George; Newman, Jerry. 2004. *Compensation — Eighth Edition*. New York: McGraw Hill.

Mulvey, Paul W.; LeBlanc, Peter V.; Heneman, Robert L. 2002. *The Knowledge of Pay Study: E-mails from the Frontline*. Scottsdale: WorldatWork.

Reynolds, Calvin. 2006. *Compensating North American Expatriates*. Scottsdale: WorldatWork.

Rubino, John A. 2004. *Communicating Compensation Programs*. Scottsdale: WorldatWork.

Sotherland, Jude. 2006. *When Pay Plans Go Wrong — Managing Compliance Issues Before the Audit*. Scottsdale: WorldatWork.

Total Rewards Glossary. 2006. Scottsdale: WorldatWork.

WorldatWork Courses (www.worldatwork.org/education)

Compensation Fundamentals

C1: Regulatory Environments for Compensation Programs

C2: Job Analysis, Documentation and Evaluation

C4/GR4: Base Pay Management

C17: Market Pricing — Conducting a Competitive Pay Analysis

T1/GR1: Total Rewards Management

T9/GR7: International Remuneration: An Overview of Global Rewards Compensation Fundamentals